CREATING MEANING

a book about culture and democracy

edited by Jerry Rothwell

VALLEY
CWM A BRO
&VALE

RECYCLED PAPER

ISBN No. 0 9514831 2 9

ACKNOWLEDGEMENTS

Whilst this publication has been collected and shaped by present Valley and Vale team members, we would like to acknowledge the contribution that twelve years of Valley and Vale staff, volunteers, workshop participants and managers have made to the development of the ideas it contains. If we thanked them all it would require a book at least twice the size, so thank you, you know who you are...

Valley and Vale gratefully acknowledges the sponsorship of D. P. & M. (Information Technology) plc. without whose support this book would not have seen the light of day.

D. P. & M. is an award winner under the Business Sponsorship Incentive Scheme for its support of this project. The BSIS is a government scheme, administered by the Association for Business Sponsorship of the Arts.

You can contact **Valley and Vale** at:

Blaengarw Workmen's Hall,
Blaengarw Road,
Blaengarw,
Nr. BRIDGEND
Mid Glamorgan
CF32 8AW
Tel. 0656-871911
Fax. 0656-870507

Holm View Centre,
Skomer Road,
Gibbonsdown,
BARRY,
South Glamorgan,
CF6 3DA
Tel. 0446-742289
Fax. 0446-738461

Printed by: Zenith Print Group, Treforest, Pontypridd, Mid Glam, CF37 5SX

Culture: The 'social heritage' of a community: the total body of material artefacts (tools, weapons, houses; places of work, worship, government, recreation; works of art, etc.); of collective mental and spiritual 'artefacts' (systems of symbols, ideas, beliefs, aesthetic perceptions, values, etc.); and of distinctive forms of behaviour (institutions, groupings, rituals, modes of organisation, etc) created by a people (sometimes deliberately, sometimes through unforeseen interconnections and consequences) in their ongoing activities within their particular life-conditions, and (through undergoing kinds and degrees of change) transmitted from generation to generation.

Democracy: A word originating in the classical Greek city states, and meaning the rule of the demos, the citizen body: the right of all to decide what are matters of general concern.

The size of modern nation states has meant that (apart from those which include provision for a referendum in their constitutions) democracy is no longer direct but indirect, i.e. through the election of representatives, and hence the term representative democracy.

Critics of democracy fall into two groups. The first is opposed to democracy, root and branch, on the grounds that it is the least efficient form of government and one in which the stability of the State is threatened by faction, complex issues are distorted by popular discussion, difficult decisions evaded or put off, and matters of judgement reduced to the lowest common denominator acceptable to a majority of voters. The second, in favour of the principles of democracy, argues that these are inadequately realised unless carried further, e.g. by extending equal rights for all citizens from the political and legal to the economic sphere, without which democracy remains at best incomplete, at worst a sham (formal democracy) disguising the reality of class rule.

A variant of this type of criticism argues that, with the growth of bureaucracy and the power of governments, decisions are no longer effectively influenced by the view of the government or the elected representatives; hence the demand for greater participation at all levels of decision-making and the problem of how to reconcile this demand with the need for prompt and effective decisions on complex and controversial issues.

from
*The Fontana Dictionary
of Modern Thought*

CREATING MEANING explores some of the issues that are raised by attempts to broaden participation in cultural activity, through looking at the development of a single organisation. Valley and Vale has been working in the Vale of Glamorgan since 1981 and in the Ogwr district since 1983. Its growth has inevitably reflected both the changing social and economic structures in Britain in general, and the tumultuous developments in South Wales in particular, in the last eleven years.

The book is based on articles written over the last decade which explore key areas of Valley and Vale's practice and relate them to a broader set of ideas. It doesn't try to be an encyclopaedia of work accomplished or a series of project reports. Instead, it aims to give an insight into how ideas about 'community arts' have developed since 1980: from its initial motivation based on the belief that participation in the arts should be a 'basic human right', towards the development of issue-based work stimulated by the desire to support specific campaigns, through to the more recent attempts to use the arts as a tool for longer term development, as part of a process of building broader local involvement in the decisions that affect the lives of our communities.

The articles are grouped into sections which aim to give an insight into the thinking which has accompanied these different ways of working:
The Prologue is a broad outline of the ideas that now underpin Valley and Vale's practice;
Striking Images looks back at work undertaken in support of particular campaigns;
Global Wales demonstrates the importance of an international cultural perspective;
Making History describes the thinking behind arts work which examines and celebrates 'people's history';
Taking Control explores issues which arise out of the use of the arts as a tool for self-advocacy;
Changing Places looks at arts activities which have empowered communities to take part in local planning;
and The Epilogue suggests the relevance of 'community arts' to current world developments.
The Chronology which runs throughout the book, aims to give a sense of what else was going on in the world, and the degree to which Valley and Vale's work reflected it.

In 1985, Owen Kelly wrote in *Community Art and the State*:

"The community arts movement...has no clear understanding of its own history. It has neither documented its own history, nor drawn any conclusions from it. Community artists have therefore failed to develop a consistent set of definitions, with the result that the movement has staggered drunkenly from one direction to another."

This is unfortunately as true now as it was then. *Creating Meaning* is part of the attempt to rectify that state of affairs, to understand where the movement has been and to contribute to and stimulate debate about where 'community arts' should be going.

**Valley and Vale,
June 1992**

PROLOGUE

Before the industrial revolution, 'art' was a term which described all activities requiring an element of skill. It could as easily be used of war, sex or felling trees as of poetry, painting and music. In the succeeding two hundred years, as Western European societies became industrialised, 'art' has come to describe a much more limited area of activity, something created by a professional artist class, accepted by critics and placed in a context which the public need to be educated to appreciate.

This process, by which the notion of 'art' shifts from being an approach to human activity - a way of seeing and doing which touches all our lives - and becomes a series of specialisms ('art forms') practised by a small minority of people, has accelerated in the twentieth century.

Culture, including the arts, is the process by which human beings make meaning in the world. The meanings we make and the knowledge we hold shape our decisions and our actions, determining the future development of human societies.

In industrial societies, the most influential meanings are developed and communicated through complex technologies. Control of these technologies is concentrated in the hands of a few powerful producers, resulting in unequal access to the tools to create and distribute ideas and information. Forms of communication which do not use these dominant distribution systems are marginalised. A hierarchy of power, based on the ownership and control of the means of cultural production, limits most people to the roles of spectator, reader, watcher and listener, rather than those of actor, broadcaster or writer. Like medicine, motor cars and food, our cultural experiences usually come fast and highly packaged.

This is not to say we are simply passive consumers. We make popular culture a resource for our own frustrated creativity, resist and re-interpret its messages, use its icons for our own ends. Through our clothes, decorations and collections we combine and give new meanings to the images our society offers. But no matter how active an audience we become, these remain essentially private strategies of survival. They have little effect on the distribution of economic and social power. Our society achieves the appearance of consent by

8

< Garw Junior Video Group, Easter Playschemes, 1991 (Garw Junior Photo Workshop)

limiting the ideas available and the voices heard, marginalising those that threaten existing power structures.

At the heart of the beliefs which underpin the work described in this book is the right of all people to have a hand in the production of their own cultural meanings and identities, in the construction of what it means to live in Barry or Blaengarw, in Britain or Bangladesh, in Ireland or El Salvador. This can only be brought about by the development of a new set of relationships between people, relationships which enable us to become both reader and writer, performer and audience, viewer and viewed.

The discovery that people who don't define themselves as artists can - given the tools and the opportunity - produce art of the highest standard should not be any surprise to us. They have been doing so for thousands of years, and it is only relatively recently that these activities have been elevated to the status of a specialised, pseudo-magical skill. Despite this, what is created in community arts workshops throughout Britain is rarely considered worthy of comment by the fraternity of art critics, where a kind of cultural apartheid which ignores the creations of the majority reigns, and for whom the very notion of 'popular arts' is a fundamental challenge to their self-appointed role as sifters of genius and arbiters of originality.

The last ten years have seen technological, political and cultural shifts as great as those in the previous one hundred. Arguably, we are now entering a phase as significant - and with as great an upheaval in patterns of life - as that of the Industrial Revolution. Technological changes place on offer the potential to create significantly new worlds - for the development of a truly participatory democracy or for the increasing centralisation of power and control. The direction we go in will be significantly influenced by cultural developments, by the meanings we make and the meanings we have access to.

It is a question finally of what kind of society we want to see developing: one where people are increasingly reliant upon mass purveyors of meaning for their information, ideas and opinions, or one where we all have access to the tools to explore and communicate our ideas and visions of the world, to become, in short, the subjects of our own lives.

PROLOGUE

Part 1 STRIKING IMAGES

MAESTEG
WOMEN
SOUTH WALES
SUPPORT
THE
MINERS

STRIKING IMAGES

Like other progressive movements which grew out of the 1960's, community arts projects in the 70's and 80's often focussed on work with people engaged in specific campaigns. Frequently, cultural activity became an important tool in addressing areas of local or national policy from the perspective of groups who - for one reason or another - did not have access to the mainstream media. People engaged in direct political struggles usually had a clear motive for using the arts: they had a message and they wanted to get it across.

This approach led both to some very effective campaigns and to some radical art, but it also had its limitations. Activities which brought people together around single issues frequently had no life beyond the issue in question. As a result, they sometimes failed to grapple with the deeper causes of a particular problem: focussing, for example, on the damp walls in a particular estate, rather than on the broader issues of how to change housing policy in the area. This was sometimes effective in bringing about short term improvements, but the projects rarely involved people in longer term participation in the decisions taken about their communities. When the immediate problem went away, so did the pressure group; and with them went the photo workshop, the video equipment, the mobile screenprinting resource.

Of all the campaigns which were supported by community arts activity in the 1980's, the miners' strike of 1984-5 was undoubtedly the most significant. It was a critical moment for people in mining communities as well as for the Trade Union movement and for Thatcherism.

The dispute generated an extensive and vibrant culture in support of the strike: photo exhibitions toured the country portraying the dispute in terms different from those in the mainstream press; theatre companies put their skills to the service of the miners; print workshops produced posters, T-shirts and badges; over a thousand copies of the Miner's Campaign Tapes - produced by members of independent video workshops - were seen by union members and support groups, the largest ever distribution of community produced video.

"We didn't want to remain invisible; we wanted to let people know that we are alive and kicking in this valley."

Meryl, Abertillery, 1985

12

< Maesteg women picketing Margam Steelworks, Port Talbot, June 1984 (Tondu Photo Workshop)

The cause of the miners united groups which had different experiences but a similar interest in the transformation of society. The strike saw imaginative, if unlikely, links between black community groups campaigning against police racism and trades unionists opposing the enforcement of anti-union legislation, between city-based lesbian and gay groups and rural miners' support groups.

Unfortunately, these new dialogues between mining communities and the diverse groups who came to support them, ceased to be a priority once the strike had ended. The defeat of the miners was not only a blow to the trade union movement, it also signalled a failure to build on these positive developments, to make the new networks part of a future notion of political activity.

For Valley and Vale, whose work had gathered momentum from the needs of communities engaged in the strike, the end of the dispute heralded a shift in priorities:

"There was a point in our work where we moved away from projects which were just about campaigning. In the 1960's and 70's you could go on a protest march and it made a difference; the government had to act if there was 50,000 people in one place saying the same thing, because there was a belief it was there to respond to the needs of the people. That politics has gone out of the window. Petitions don't work any more. The government doesn't believe it has to respond to people's demands. That's why we moved away from making campaign videos and started working with a wider, longer-term, less spontaneous concept of change."

Phil Cope
Valley and Vale

CHRONOLOGY

1979

May 3: Margaret Thatcher wins general election.

*In the same month, **discussions** are under way between community and youth workers in the rural Vale of Glamorgan to set up a **community arts team**.*

1980

Jan 17: British Steel announce they will be cutting 11,287 jobs in Wales by the end of March.

May 1: Ian McGregor named as Chairman of British Steel.

Sep 22: Solidarity is formed in Poland.

Oct 10: "*The Lady's not for turning*" (Margaret Thatcher, Conservative Party conference).

Oct 26: 60,000 protesters take part in the biggest anti-nuclear demonstration for twenty years.

Nov 4: Ronald Reagan defeats Jimmy Carter in the US Presidential election.

Nov 10: Michael Foot becomes Labour Party leader.

Dec 3: The Thatcher government abolishes 192 quangos, bringing the total number she has wound up since coming to power to 400.

Dec 8: John Lennon shot dead by Mark Chapman.

*In September 1980, a nine month **pilot project** was established to explore the feasibility of a permanent community arts team serving the rural Vale of Glamorgan.*

1981

Jan 20: Reagan inaugurated as the 40th US president.

Jan 27: Rupert Murdoch buys *The Times*.

Feb 10: Coal Board announces plans to close 50 pits employing 30,000 miners.

Feb 17: South Wales miners begin unofficial strike in protest at planned closures.

Mar 26: SDP launched.

>>

Lessons from the Miners' Strike

"For the majority of people in Britain, the miners' strike of 1984-5 was experienced second hand, through the media. For those involved directly in the strike it soon became clear that the events in which they were participating, on picket lines and in their communities, were being exaggerated, ignored or distorted in the papers and on TV and radio. Their story wasn't being told. The news media established an agenda - of secret ballots, picket line violence and personalities - which avoided the central issues in the strike.

The Fleet Street press in particular adopted a consistently hostile attitude to the NUM. To understand why this happened, it is necessary to look at the issue of ownership and control. The number of national newspapers has been shrinking steadily since the 1920's, and most of those to disappear have been on the left (for example *The Daily Herald* and *The News Chronicle*). At the time of the strike, the national press was dominated by three men - Rupert Murdoch, Robert Maxwell and Victor Matthews - who between them controlled 74.5% of the total circulation.

The manufacture and distribution of 'news' forms only part of the interests of the multinational companies who own most of the press. Many of these companies also have stakes in banks, oil companies and the nuclear industry. Sixteen of the leading newspapers in Wales, including *The Western Mail* and *The South Wales Echo*, are owned by Thompson Regional Newspapers, part of the International Thompson Organisation, whose interests include petroleum holdings and North Sea oil.

These economic interests have a direct influence on the editorial policies of the press. The political loyalties of individual newspapers are dependent on those of its owners. Indeed, control over editorial policy is an important factor in the desire of press barons to own national newspapers (which are not always the most profitable way of investing capital). As Victor Matthews, owner of *The Daily Express*, has said: "By and large, the editors will have complete freedom as long as they agree with the policy I have laid down."

The popular press tended not to publish the reasons why miners were on strike or investigate the role of the government in provoking the dispute or the extent of support for the strike or the behaviour of the police. Instead, propagandist articles such *The Sun's* 'Mine Fuhrer' headline (15th May 1984) and the spoof Scargill

Valley and Vale had been working in the mining communities of the Ogwr district for about a year before the start of the dispute, having made the move from a base in the rural Vale of Glamorgan to Tondu at the meeting point of the three Ogwr valleys.

This article, written in 1985, attempted to draw some lessons from the work undertaken during the strike for future cultural activity in support of campaigns.

'confession' - 'The Truth That Scargill Dare Not Tell' - in *The Daily Express* (9th May 1984) attempted to undermine the credibility of the NUM leadership and played their part in reducing public support for striking miners.

> *The Sun,* 15th May 1984

Television played a similar, though sometimes less direct role. Broadcasting institutions are, like the press, an integral part of the British establishment. Unlike newspapers, broadcasting companies avoid a stated party loyalty. However, the government appoints the governors of both the BBC and the IBA, and in the case of the BBC, the Chair of the Governors is appointed on the advice of the Home Office. Individual companies are not democratically accountable either in their structure or decision-making processes. Despite this, there remains a belief in the impartiality of the broadcast media. Both the IBA and the BBC claim to have a commitment to 'balance', and indeed there were instances during the strike when the case of striking miners was given air time. However, particularly in relation to news output, this notion of 'balance' needs to be questioned. For although the NCB and the NUM may have been given equal coverage in terms of hours of broadcasting, and although NUM officials may have been sought out by reporters and current affairs programmes to give their views, the context in which the NUM arguments were put frequently undermined what they had to say. Len Masterman, analysed this process at work in the BBC coverage of Orgreave in June 1984:

> "...the differential credibility accorded to police representatives and miners as sources is revealing. The miner's eye-witness story is dismissed as astonishing, while the police spokesperson is asked in all seriousness for his assessment of a situation at which he was not present. Similarly, the police statement that Scargill 'slipped' in injuring his head, far from being challenged by reporters, is privileged against Scargill's mere 'claims' that he was struck by a riot shield."

>> 1981

Apr 4: Riots in Brixton.

Apr 11: Bobby Sands wins Fermanagh & South Tyrone By-election.

Apr 23: Unemployment reaches 2.5 million.

May 5: Bobby Sands dies after hunger strike.

May 8: Ken Livingstone elected leader of GLC.

May 11: Bob Marley dies.

May 30: People's March for Jobs reaches London, but is refused entry to Whitehall.

July 2: Government announces cuts in University grants.

July 5: Riots in Toxteth, London, Birmingham, Preston, Hull, Wolverhampton and Ellesmere Port.

July 29: Royal Wedding: Prince Charles marries Lady Diana Spencer.

Aug 5: Heseltine announces package for depressed areas of Merseyside.

Aug 7: One million Solidarity members go on strike in protest at Polish food and economic crisis.

Sep 27: Denis Healey defeats Tony Benn in Labour Deputy Leadership contest.

Oct 3: Hunger strike in Belfast formally ends after seven months and ten deaths.

Oct 12: British Leyland announces closure of three plants, losing 2,850 jobs.

Oct 15: "*My father did not riot, he got on his bike and looked for work*" (Norman Tebbit).

Oct 24: 150,000 people march to Hyde Park to protest at presence of Cruise Missiles on British soil.

Dec 8: Arthur Scargill elected President of NUM.

Dec 28: Women's Peace Camp established at Greenham Common.

*The **Vale of Glamorgan Community Arts Team** started work on 20 **July 1981, based at St. Donat's Arts Centre** and initially **funded for 12 months** by the MSC.*

>>

Television news identifies itself as an integral part of parliamentary democracy. It portrays competing views of an issue so long as those views are seen as being part of the consensus. Those who offer a challenge to the consensus, and to the decisions Parliament makes in its name, as striking miners did, are likely to be characterised as against the national interest ('the enemy within') and broadcasters see it as legitimate or even necessary to cast doubt on what they have to say. The NUM found it difficult to turn the debate away from the agenda proposed by the media to the central issues involved: the place of coal in a safe energy policy, the democratic control of industry, the social and cultural importance of the coal-mining communities themselves.

Misrepresentation by a hostile press had a significant effect on communities which were directly involved in the strike. Firstly, there was a growing awareness of the way the news media distorted events. Secondly, there was a recognition that the media would play a crucial role in the success or failure of the strike and that there was a need to find alternative means of getting their voices heard. This realisation generated the biggest growth of arts activity in support of union struggle in recent history, and certainly since the birth of the community arts movement.

> Coal lorries, M4, 1984 (Tondu Photo Workshop)

One example of this activity was the work of **Tondu Photo Workshop** in Mid Glamorgan, which was originally set up as a photography facility for local unemployed young people by Valley and Vale in 1983. It soon became apparent that members should and could run the workshop for themselves as an autonomous body, and it was as such that it was approached by the local lodge of the NUM in 1984. The first requests were very basic ones: to photograph the number-plates of lorries transporting coal across picket lines.

This use of photography as a record was almost enough to close the project down, and Valley and Vale with it. A front page headline appeared in the local paper ('Yes, we took M4 pictures for NUM'), and a lesser report in *The Times*. The local Tory MP, Peter Hubbard-Miles, wanted to know why state funds were being used for 'political' purposes:

"Men in power always endeavour to extend their power. The tendency of every government is to despotism. And in this even the best governments must end, if the people are not vigilant and determined to resist abuses as soon as they begin. Whenever a people cease to reason about their rights and to be awake to encroachments, they are in danger of being enslaved."

Dr. Richard Price of Llangeinor, Garw Valley, 1789

"I don't consider that party politics are in common with education. If they are talking about politics as a subject, it is alright, but when the subject becomes purely partisan it is out of the sphere of art...There must be insurance that any future grant is used for art education, and not for political purposes in a political strike."

> Fundraising poster, Dec. 1984 (Tondu Photo Workshop)

This simple and very practical use of photography developed into the production of two widely distributed posters, one of which ('Merry Xmas') was based on a photograph of children in front of a pit which was due to close. The caption asked for money, food and toys for the children of striking miners over the Christmas period. The poster was important in that it was produced in co-operation with the NUM lodge, with decisions on the location, the final image, text and design being made collectively.

Collaboration of this kind between arts groups and the mineworkers' union did not follow a coolly thought out strategy. Whilst the adhoc nature of much of the supporting activity surrounding the strike generated a tremendous sense of excitement, it meant that there was initially a need to reach a common understanding of what role cultural work might play in the strike. As one of the collective, Pete Bullock, said of the 'Merry Xmas' poster:

"The image used on this poster was in many ways a throwback to the 'helpless appeal' of the Oxfam and Shelter campaigns of the 60's and early 70's. We realise that we should have been working with the unions in times of 'peace' and developing a new visual language...It is too late to experiment with this new language during this dispute, as results have to be immediate."

However, the continuing involvement with the lodge encouraged several striking miners to join the workshop, which began producing more challenging images of the dispute from their point of view. From this work came an exhibition, **A Few Hotheads**, which toured nationally but dealt with the specific issues of the strike as they related to the Llynfi valley. The exhibition was a conscious attempt to present a picture which differed both from the

>> 1981

*Projects that year included a summer playscheme **All In A Day's Work**, **The Jungle Room** - a mural, **The Haunted House** - a residency by Paupers' Carnival Theatre Company, and **Crow** - a large-scale street event on Nov 5th.*

1982

Jan 5: Mark Thatcher goes missing in the Sahara, but is found two days later.

Jan 26: Unemployment reaches 3 million.

Jan 30: Riots in St. Paul's area of Bristol.

Feb 28: Geoffrey Boycott leads rebel cricket tour of South Africa.

Mar 4: Barbican Centre opens.

Mar 15: Michael Bogdanov goes on trial for his production of The Romans in Britain. The trial is stopped 3 days later.

Mar 19: Argentinian scrap metal dealers land in South Georgia and plant the Argentine flag.

Mar 28: Iranians gain ground in heaviest fighting in Gulf War.

Apr 2: Argentina captures Falkland Islands/Malvinas.

Apr 3: UN backs Britain's Falklands protest.

May 2: Belgrano sunk.

May 29: Battle of Goose Green.

May 29: Pope John Paul visits Britain.

Jun 6: Israel invades Lebanon.

Jun 14: Argentinians surrender Falklands.

Jun 17: Galtieri ousted.

Jul 20: IRA bombings in Hyde and Regent parks.

Aug 4: 250 killed in Bierut as Israelis send in forces.

conventional news output and from the tradition of 'social documentary' photographs of working class life. One of the participants said of the exhibition:

> "We tried to put over an alternative point of view to the media by showing all aspects of fundraising: marches, rallies, morale-boosting carnivals, as well as the picket lines."

This image of the strike, one in which people were actively organising to defend their communities, was seen as more threatening than the portrayals in the media of

<
Rally and march,
Port Talbot,
April 1984
(Tondu Photo Workshop)

'Scargill's stormtroopers' and passive victims. Hubbard-Miles viewed the exhibition as intimidatory:

> "This exhibition was certainly political....I can understand photos of miners in groups or families and the sort of dismay they are suffering...indeed, I have a great deal of sympathy. But when it involves political intimidation I have no sympathy at all."

Whilst on display at The Brewery Arts Centre in Kendal, governors and trustees attempted to have the exhibition removed, finally settling for a disclaimer distancing the views of the workshop from those of the arts centre. Comments from the centre's visitor's book indicate how the exhibition acted to stir debate not just about the photographs themselves, but about the wider issues in the strike, in a non-mining area.

The work of the Tondu Photo Workshop, like the many

18

other examples of cultural activity stimulated by the strike, raises fundamental questions about the representation of working class people, particularly those directly involved in an industrial dispute.

There is a clear need to develop an alternative system of producing and distributing words and images, one which does not rely on a mass media controlled by capitalist economic and political interests. Even when a community's voice gains a rare national hearing, the mechanisms of broadcast TV or the national press assure a passive and isolated audience. Relying on these forms of distribution ignores the potential of empowering and activating hundreds of small, closely-linked groups through community-based work.

What was different about the exhibitions produced at the workshop was that their production was controlled by the people whose experience they described. The existence of the Photo Workshop enabled the group not only to gain a sufficient level of skill to make these images effective; it also provided the space and facilities to explore alternatives to many of the images made by the professional cultural producers of the left. The history of the representation of working, unemployed or striking people and the communities in which they live, is dominated by images of victims: poor, helpless, oppressed people needing aid or pity. Even those who have professed to support their cause have failed to see the long-term damage these portrayals cause or the potential of a different kind of imagery to inspire movements for social change.

Since 1979, the Thatcher government, aided by Saatchi and Saatchi, has had a monopoly on the images and rhetoric of a better life. There was a recognition by those involved in the miners' dispute that images showing their side of the story had to be distributed nationally and had to contain a vision of a different kind of society. Unlike the images produced by Saatchi and Saatchi, they had to have very firm roots within the experiences of the majority of people. The miners' strike demonstrated the need to reclaim the propositional nature of community activity, to argue for a vision of the future instead of taking up defensive positions. When people take action against oppression it is a vision (expressed or only half-conscious) which brings them together; a vision that is based on common experience, and on the knowledge which that experience brings. The role of any cultural movement must be to stimulate and express these visions. ▐▌

based on an article in 'Radical Wales', 1985

>> 1982

Sep 18: Lebanese Christian militia massacre hundreds in Palestinian refugee camps.

Oct 8: Thatcher tells Tory conference: *"the NHS is safe in our hands"*.

Nov 1: S4C is launched.

Nov 2: Channel 4 goes on air.

Nov 10: Leonid Brezhnev dies.

Nov 30: Animal welfare militia send letter bomb to Thatcher which explodes in Downing Street.

Dec 2: William Whitelaw complains about Channel 4 programmes giving too much air time to gay men and lesbians.

Dec 12: 20,000 women encircle Greenham Common.

*In 1982, Vale of Glamorgan Community Arts extended its work from rural areas to **Barry**. By now workshops were being offered in **dance, music, video** and **photography** (notably a youth photography workshop in Barry), visual arts and drama/theatre; these included a summer playscheme, **The Patch**. Visiting performers included **7:84, Unity Too** and **Open Cast** theatre companies. The team organised the first **Wales Community Arts Conference** and the first **Vale of Glamorgan Festival of Dance**.*

1983

Jan 14: Police shoot Stephen Waldorf, wrongly believing him to be an escaped prisoner.

Jan 17: BBC Breakfast TV begins.

Feb 3: Unemployment stands at a record 3,224,715.

Feb 9: Shergar is kidnapped. A £2 million ransom is demanded.

Feb 11: Civil servant Denis Nilson charged with murdering 17 people.

Feb 20: 600 Moslems massacred in India.

Feb 28: Yorkshire and South Wales miners called out on strike.

Mar 3: NUM executive calls strike ballot.

>>

Part 2 GLOBAL WALES

In 1992, we are being encouraged to commemorate Columbus' arrival in the Americas. The celebrations ask us to do more than remember a specific European explorer; they invite us to share in and perpetuate a particular version of the present and an ideal for the future.

The US government has spent a decade in preparation for 1992. Meanwhile in Spain and Portugal a series of festivals, including Seville's Expo 92 and events in Barcelona, Madrid and Lisbon, aim to link the Columbus 'celebrations' to the removal of European trade barriers. In the Dominican Republic, which currently faces an external debt of more than $4.2 billion and where three quarters of the rural population is malnourished, the government have spent $250 million on a lighthouse commemorating the explorer, and bulldozed the homes of one hundred thousand of its poorest people to 'beautify' the capital city. Central to the worldwide celebrations has been the promotion of the character of Columbus himself - as an intrepid self-made man, the model capitalist entrepreneur whose explorations mark the end of the inward-looking and superstitious old world, and the start of the new.

Meanwhile a counter celebration - and one with considerably less financial backing - is using the quincentennial to celebrate a different history. The '500 Years of Resistance' campaign reminds us of the ongoing struggle of indigenous American peoples to maintain their cultures and autonomy in the face of their continuing erosion by European, Japanese and US domination.

The 'discovery' of gold and silver in Latin America set in motion the enslavement of the native people by European 'conquistadors', firstly in the mines, and later in the fields and factories of the whole continent. In 1492, the population of the Americas was 110 million; a century later it had been reduced to 20 million. More than half died as a direct result of new diseases introduced by the colonists. A significant proportion of the remainder were massacred whilst refusing to accept the white man's god or his methods of social organisation. Following the destruction of indigenous tribes, the African continent was opened up to the slave trade, to provide cheap labour for the new rulers.

"The more local something is, the more universal it is."

Joan Miro

22

<Shikisha at Holm View Centre, Barry, July 1990 (as part of the *South Wales/South Africa 2* Festival)

In the atmosphere of the new world order, the Columbus quincentennial invites us to ignore this history and ally ourselves with a Euro-American ideal of progress which denies the experience of nine-tenths of the world's population. To this day the resources of the Americas are being bled dry by a debt of $440 billion to banks in North America and Europe.

In Wales, our own relationship to the rest of the world and to the experience of colonialism is complex and contradictory. As in Latin America and Africa, the Welsh nation has experienced military and economic invasion by a more powerful neighbour, followed by the suppression of indigenous culture and language. But, although itself a colonised nation, the Welsh people (as British subjects) have been partners in much of Britain's colonial exploits in Latin America, Africa and Australia. This dual relationship - of colonised and coloniser - continues into the present. We live, increasingly, in a global economy in which decisions made by governments and transnational companies relate our own destiny to the lives and experiences of people in other countries.

Understanding these connections is crucial to understanding our futures. For any cultural organisation, making links with people from other nations enables us to discover and act upon the things we hold in common, in particular to explore cultural responses to common economic, social and political problems.

There has been an international dimension to Valley and Vale's work since 1986, with the development of relationships with cultural groups abroad and the organisation of international festivals, exhibitions and workshops, which aim to link the experiences of other cultures to those of people in Wales.

This first-hand exchange of ideas, information and support is a powerful antidote to the myths and distortions we are taught to hold about other cultures, and which cement the things that divide us. The breadth of these networks is their source of strength. A global culture requires a global response.

Mar 10: Shipyard workers in Gdansk demand restoration of Solidarity.

Mar 15: Budget cuts taxes by £2 billion.

Apr 4: Gunmen get away with £7 million from Security Express van, the biggest cash robbery in British history.

Apr 14: Reagan denies that sending covert aid to Nicaraguan rebels is illegal.

Apr 19: Car bomb destroys US embassy in Bierut.

Apr 22: After release from prison, Lech Walesa returns to work at Lenin shipyard.

Apr 27: Reagan appeals to Congress to support increased aid to El Salvadorean government.

May 14: Mount Etna erupts.

Jun 11: Thatcher wins General Election with a 144 majority.

Jun 12: Michael Foot resigns as Labour leader.

Jun 13: Roy Jenkins resigns as leader of SDP.

Jun 14: Thousands of people take part in protests in Chile against General Pinochet.

Jul 6: Government announces rise in defence spending.

Jul 28: House of Representatives vote to end covert aid to Nicaraguan rebels.

Aug 6: US sends aid to Chad against Libyans.

Aug 21: Benigno Aquino assassinated in Manila.

Sep 1: Ian McGregor takes over as chairman of National Coal Board.

Oct 2: Neil Kinnock elected leader of Labour Party.

Oct 5: Cecil Parkinson admits to Sara Keays affair.

Oct 7: Thatcher announces plans to abolish GLC and metropolitan counties.

Oct 20: Armed forces seize power in Grenada.

>>

Promises, Promises

A large number of socially-concerned movements resulted, or received a major boost, from the liberal experiments of the 1960's - the peace movement (CND), the environmental movements (Friends of The Earth, Greenpeace), the women's movement, the black movement, and last, and most certainly least of all...community arts.

All the others are on the national agenda.. They receive daily coverage by the media and are discussed seriously, if not always sympathetically. Community arts is not. For the majority of the population in Britain today it does not exist.

The Fontana Dictionary of Modern Thought - usually a reliable and accurate source - offers the following description of community arts:

> *"COMMUNITY ARTS: An English term, coined about 1970 for the activities of groups of (primarily visual) artists attempting to work largely with and for local authorities, schools, remedial institutions and other communal bodies rather than the art market. Among media commonly used are mime, costume, movement, games, live and recorded music and the use of INFLATABLES."*

This isn't a particularly accurate or useful definition for community artists, but it does give an insight into how (when at all) we are perceived by the outside world.

According to Fontana, what are the areas we work in? "Mime, costume, movement, games, live and recorded music, and the use of INFLATABLES". Are these activities relevant to Britain in 1984? And who do we work with? Principally institutions, it would seem. Our aims? Not clear, but something to do with opposing the 'art market'!

Clearly nothing very significant there. By this definition, community arts doesn't appear to be a terribly important aspect of regional, national or international life, which is surprising if one listens to the very large claims made by community artists concerning the value of their work:

- we make 'the arts more accessible and relevant';

- we promote 'notions of cultural democracy';

- we effect 'social change through the development and expansion of cultural expression',

A frustration with community arts activities and thinking in 1984 led to this article by Phil Cope, which urged the movement (then represented by a rather moribund Shelton Trust) to re-examine its aims and to evaluate more realistically its successes and failures. Significantly, it was to examples of 'people's art' in other countries that the article looked for inspiration.

(and all this from just one single page of Su Braden's introduction to *Artists and People*).

In reality, however, if we're honest, there is little evidence of community arts playing a significant part in any kind of radical social change in this country since the genesis of the movement. How much of an influence can we claim to be having on racism, sexism, nationalism, class or poverty? How far is our work actively promoting equality, freedom...expression even? On the contrary, much that passes for community arts today actually bolsters the status quo, discourages dissent, acts like an acceptable soft police force.

If you share this analysis, there are at least two possible conclusions:

1. Art can't do anything significant in this area - it isn't that kind of animal. It deals with emotions and feelings, and doesn't function when too closely aligned with political action or ideas;

or

2. Perhaps we're not doing it right?

CHINA 1976-9

On the 8th January 1976, Premier Chou-En-Lai, China's only modern and unblemished popular hero, died. His death acted not only as a catalyst for the examination of his own moderate life and popular policies, but also for that of Mao Tse Tung's contribution to China's past, and its relationship to the 'Gang of 4's' present unpopular leadership.

During the month of March, thousands of people placed poems and wreaths on the Revolutionary Martyrs Memorial in the centre of Peking in Chou's honour. The square became the focal point for a living popular idea whose originator was dead. This veneration reached its height on 4th April - a traditional day of remembrance known as 'The Festival of Sweeping of the Graves'. Not surprisingly the focus of that year's Festival was Chou.

By the evening the square was crowded with people wishing to honour their dead leader. The situation was declared to be dangerous and the 'security' forces were ordered in to clear the memorial. By the time the crowds had arrived the following day, the government had cordoned off the whole square in order to discourage a repetition of the previous day's demonstrations of strong

Oct 30: Earthquake in Turkey kills 2,000.

Nov 3: Referendum of white South Africans results in a vote to share power with 'coloureds' and Indians but not blacks.

Dec 10: Raul Alfonsin becomes Argentina's first civilian president for 8 years.

Dec 17: IRA bomb explodes outside Harrods.

In 1983 the team continued its programme of **regular workshops,** *including its first workshops in* **the valleys and Bridgend,** *with video playing an increasingly important role.* **Sticks & Stones,** *a street event based on the life of St. Illtyd, patron saint of Llantwit Major, took place in November.*

1984

Jan 2: A new report reveals acid rain is seriously contaminating Britain's lakes and rivers.

Jan 2: Government bans union membership at GCHQ.

Jan 9: Sarah Tisdall charged under Official Secrets Act.

Feb 9: Soviet leader Yuri Andropov dies; Konstantin Chernenko succeeds him.

Feb 14: Ice-skaters Torvill and Dean win Olympic gold.

Mar 5: Scientists warn of the 'greenhouse effect'.

Mar 12: Miners' strike begins.

Apr 1: Marvin Gaye shot dead by his father.

Apr 4: 300 police clear main peace camp at Greenham Common.

Apr 22: WPC Yvonne Fletcher shot dead outside Libyan embassy.

May 8: Soviet Union boycotts Olympics.

May 24: Nicaragua announces first elections since 1979.

May 29: Riot police battle miners at Orgreave.

Jun 15: Miner picketing Yorkshire power station killed by scab lorry.

>>

popular feeling. Angry scenes ensued, the focus of which turned from the veneration of Chou to a criticism of the present leadership of the 'Gang of 4'. The police moved in and arrests began, following which it is estimated that between two and four thousand people were immediately executed. The events of April 5th were thenceforth known as the Tiananmen Incident, which became a symbol of resistance for the Chinese people.

In September of that year, Mao died, to be followed in the next month by the inevitable fall of the 'Gang of 4', which included Mao's widow, Chiang Ching. A period of new 'liberalism' was the result, culminating two years later in the reversal of the 'counter-revolutionary' verdict previously imposed upon the Tiananmen Incident. As a result, the events of April 5th 1976 were officially vindicated and the Democracy Movement, as it came to be known, was born.

The Movement was centred on 'Democracy Wall', a free speech area in the centre of Peking and the scene of spontaneous mass meetings and demonstrations. This period saw an explosion in the number of unofficial presses and wall posters, demanding human rights and criticising the system.

The call for democracy was twofold - both political and cultural. Politics and art were seen as two necessary sides of the same coin in their struggle. These dual aims of the Democracy Movement are clear from the manifesto of one of the many small presses, the 'April 5th Study Group':

> "To publish the people's thoughts and words which for all kinds of reasons are not contained in official publications. To publish popular literature which develops the spirit of April 5th."

The Democracy Movement represented the right to contribute to the debate about the decisions which were being taken on your behalf, to contribute...and to self-expression.

The first editorial of the magazine *Today* stated:

> "Now our generation can sing the song that's been in our hearts for ten long years...today, as people open their eyes anew, we should never again take such a narrow view of 9,000 years of cultural heritage, but to start to use a broader perspective to survey the surrounding horizons. Only in this way can we rediscover our own value".

The arts, and in particular poetry, became an integral part of the Democracy Movement's activities. Poems were declaimed on the streets of Peking, on Democracy Wall, on huge posters, and in the many unofficial presses. Indeed, the Democracy Movement's protests came principally through poetry - made accessible by public display and reciting. And this poetry came, not from the intellectuals and established artists, but rather from people involved in the struggle for a say in their own lives.

What's interesting about the many poems that were composed during this period is the observable improvement in standards from the banal propagandist early work:

> "Let's go forwards hand in hand
> March towards the bright dawning.
> The early morning sunlight chases the fog
> away,
> On 'Democracy Wall'
> The People have shown their strength."

(from 'Dawn' by a Peking worker, published in *April 5th Forum*, December 1978)

to the more subtle and effective verses created as the Movement developed in confidence:

> "The low sweeping pitchblack curtain of night
> uses its strong sturdy chest
> to push down the head of the great sea
> trying to suffocate its freedom to breathe;
> and the great sea is actually so silent
> that it seems to have already submitted to the darkness...
>
> The great sea raises its head aloft and puffs out its chest,
> It is going to roar out in anger once again!"

(from 'The Great Sea' published in *Live*, April 1979)

Although this poem may seem simple in its allegory, the rapid improvement even this work demonstrates as compared with the earlier example suggests the possibility of the development of a really effective art to serve the changing needs of its people, had the movement not been prematurely and aggressively curtailed by the authorities.

The Democracy Movement lasted only from November 1978 until May 1979, but in that short time it demonstrated the potential power of the written and spoken word in the service of people's political aspirations. A leading figure of the Democracy Movement wrote, just prior to his imprisonment:

>> 1984

Jul 9: Fire damages York Minster. It is suggested that this is evidence of God's disapproval of Bishop of Durham's views on the Resurrection.

Jul 12: Robert Maxwell buys Mirror Group.

Jul 23: Government enquiry says radiation from Sellafield is not cause of high cancer rate in local children.

Aug 18: Clive Ponting charged under Official Secrets Act, for his revelations about the sinking of the *Belgrano*.

Sep 12: High Court grants eviction order against Greenham Common peace camp.

Oct 12: IRA bomb Grand Hotel in Brighton during Conservative Party Conference.

Oct 31: Indira Gandhi assassinated.

Nov 6: High Court declares Miners' Strike is illegal and fines NUM £200,000.

Nov 6: Reagan is re-elected as US president.

Nov 30: Two miners charged with murdering minicab driver.

Dec 10: Leak from chemical factory kills 2,000 at Bhopal.

Dec 19: Britain and China sign treaty returning Hong Kong to China in 1997.

Also in 1984: 'yuppie' comes into English language.

In 1984, Vale of Glamorgan Community Arts changed its name to **Valley and Vale Community Arts,** *following the move from St. Donat's Arts Centre to a new base in* **Tondu Old Junior School** *at the base of the Garw, Llynfi and Ogmore valleys.*

Work included the **Three Valleys Festival** *and summer playschemes, the establishment of* **distribution networks** *for videos and exhibitions through the libraries service and the establishment of the* **Tondu Photo Workshop.** *Sponsorship from Sony resulted in an increase in video productions, including* **Trying To Connect You** *- a video about vandalism, and* **The Evidence I Shall Give** *- a documentary produced by probationers in Maesteg.*

>>

"They rely on their 'invincible' dictatorship of blood and iron, and yet a few little sheets of paper and a few lines of writing, a few shouts and they're frightened out of their wits."

MEXICO 1910-1940

In September 1910, the ruling classes celebrated 100 years of Mexico's 'independence' and the 're-election' of Porfiro Diaz, the eighty year old dictator who had run a police state in a country of poverty and oppression since 1884. The celebrations, which included for the first time 'ancient and ethnic' arts - inadvertently started a cultural revolution which developed into an attack on Diaz's leadership and his eventual removal a year later.

Recognising the people's art in the celebration of Mexico's cultural tradition focussed attention on the working class, past and present. The cultural revolution, which resulted from Diaz's expensive birthday party, developed into an assault on the status quo. The artistic and political revolutions of Mexico were simultaneous and interdependent.

One of the leaders of the movement, David Alfaro Siqueiros, wrote:

"Our work is determined by historical social causes. It is an integral, living part of a collective, intellectual movement, of a common aesthetic drive, which developed along with our collective national political aspirations."

<
Dream of a Sunday Afternoon in the Alameda,
fresco by Diego Rivera,
1947-8

The toppling of Diaz in 1911 preceded nine long years of internal struggle for a free Mexico. In 1920, when the popular General Alvaro Obregon - farmer turned soldier - became president, the promised reforms began in earnest. Mexican artists who had previously either fought in the revolutionary armies or been forced into exile actively participated in the social and cultural reconstruction of their country.

Orozco, Rivera, Tamayo and Siqueiros, the principal muralists, focussed their work primarily on the 1910 revolution. Their political activism and their artistic work went hand-in-hand. Art for them was a weapon in the armoury of Mexico's struggle. Leon Trotsky said of their work:

> *"Do you wish to know what revolutionary art is like? Look at the frescoes of Rivera...You have before you, not simply a painting, an object of passive, aesthetic contemplation, but a living part of the class struggle."*

> *Man, Controller of the Universe, Diego Rivera, 1934*

The Mexican Muralist movement developed five rules for their work, rules which are still worth studying closely by those of us who are concerned about the social significance of cultural work.

1. Their murals were collectively developed, from idea to implementation. This they felt would result in a product which best represented community needs as well as uniting the creators.

2. They believed that no work could be effective without a clear guiding policy - the importance of theory.

3. They advocated the use of all modern tools, materials and techniques available. Theirs was a scientific approach which rejected the image of the artist as romantic fossil.

4. Their aim was to satisfy a local need for their murals as well as reflecting national and international issues. Their work was not to be parochial. It had to have national significance to be really effective.

5. They believed their images should speak clearly and concisely...and thus powerfully.

>> 1984

There was an increased involvement in national organisations including the **Federation of Community Photography Workshops,** *the* **South Wales Association of Community Arts**, *and the* **Shelton Trust,** *which in 1984 launched its* **Campaign For Cultural Democracy.**

1985

Feb 20: Thatcher tells US congress that she supports 'Star Wars' program.

Feb 25: 3,807 miners go back to work.

Feb 25: Teachers' pay dispute begins.

Mar 3: Miners' Strike ends.

Mar 11: Mikhail Gorbachev becomes new Soviet leader after death of Chernenko.

Apr 30: Reagan announces plans for total trade embargo on elected Sandinista regime in Nicaragua.

May 11: Fire at Bradford City football ground kills 40.

May 29: Liverpool fans riot at Heysel Stadium in Brussels, resulting in 41 deaths.

Jun 1: 300 arrested from 'Peace Convoy' heading for Stonehenge.

Jun 2: UEFA bans English football clubs from playing in Europe.

Jul 7: Live Aid concert.

Jul 10: The Greenpeace ship, *Rainbow Warrior*, is damaged by a bomb planted by French secret service in New Zealand.

Jul 16: Local Government Bill abolishing GLC becomes law.

Jul 21: Botha announces state of emergency in 30 districts in South Africa, where more than a year of unrest has left 500 dead.

Sept 18: Opinion polls put the SDP/Liberal Alliance in the lead by 9.5% over Labour with the Tories third.

Sep 23: Rupert Murdoch buys 20th Century Fox.

Sep 26: Government announces £1 million to be spent on countering AIDS.

>>

The Mexican muralists saw their paintings as part of a long tradition of clear, concrete ideological art from Egyptian and Greek through to Byzantine and Renaissance art, effectively deflating the criticism of those who dismissed their work on the grounds of its political or ideological nature.

<
The Great City of Tenochtitlan ,
fresco by Diego Rivera,
1945

Siqueiros puts it clearly:

"Is it really possible to believe...that concrete political expression cannot be artistic and that the only true source of art is abstruse and poetic? This is a lie...invented by the enemies of social art; they say that the great art of the past has always been obscure and not concrete or ideological. Was Egyptian mythology obscure?..or the mythology of Greece and the Mayas and Incas? Was the dogmatic subject matter of the Christians during the Middle Ages, of the Byzantines, the Goths, of Cimabue, Giotto, Massaccio, etc, was that obscure? Was the religious painting of the Renaissance, which gave rise to the Reformation, obscure? Was the religious art of colonial Mexico obscure? Never! It was both clear and specific."

These are just two examples of the arts working successfully in periods of struggle in the service of working people. There are many other examples one could cite, mostly from outside Britain: the work of Mikis Theodorakis, the composer and political activist who opposed the generals in Greece; Victor Jara of the Chilean Folk Movement, a leader in the fight against the junta; Georg Grosz, the German artist who foresaw the coming of Hitler and Fascism; Garcia Lorca, the popular poet and folk hero of Spain; Ictus Theatre Company in Santiago; Pablo Neruda, the Chilean Communist Party leader and poet.

Whether you would describe any of the above individuals as community artists or any of the work they were/are involved in as 'community arts', depends on your definition of its varied manifestations. What is certainly true, however, is that they all were or are successful to a greater or lesser degree in connecting with the popular consciousness of working people through the exercise of their particular art forms. And as Janet Wolff writes in *The Social Production Of Art*:

> *"It is popular consciousness which is essential to the stability of our present society, and which is also vital to any ideological change, from the recognition and rejection of sexism to the understanding of the class nature of society."*

The examples quoted were not only <u>on</u> the national agenda within their respective countries, they were actively participating in the writing of that agenda. Could that be said of the community arts movement in Britain? How concerned is our work with the issues of central importance in Britain today? Only by such direct contact between the real needs and issues of concern to people and the facilitating skills of arts workers will community arts become respected as more than a mere leisure time alternative.

The Conservative Government won the 1983 election on a better understanding of the use of clear imagery, a more practical knowledge of the strength of the spoken and written word, as well as the ownership or control of the main means of disseminating these words and images. At the same time, the Labour Party was offering black and white posters of young people being swept down the drain. Perhaps our role should be in helping to create clearer, and more effective images for and of the left, with the community it is attempting to serve. ▌▌

published in 'Another Standard', (journal of The Shelton Trust), Autumn, 1984

> Tiananmen Square, October 1989 (Phil Cope)

>> 1985

Sep 28: Riots in Brixton and Handsworth.

Oct 1: Riots in Toxteth and Peckham.

Oct 7: Broadwater Farm riot.

Nov 19: Reagan and Gorbachev begin strategic arms limitation talks in Geneva.

Nov 27: Anglo-Irish agreement is signed.

In 1985 Valley and Vale's work included production of two videos by people with disabilities, **You Got Me Thinking** *and* **Disability/Capability***, a* **Festival of Dance** *including performances by Phoenix Dance Company and Barry Boys Comprehensive School, the* **Garw Valley Project** *- a multi-media portrayal of the valley, and a continuing programme of* **arts and training workshops.** *The team moved to a new base in the* **Blaengarw Workmen's Hall** *and established a membership system and a* **new constitutional and management structure.**

The team continued to work in the Vale of Glamorgan area as well as in Ogwr.

The Tondu Photo Workshop expanded, setting up as an independent organisation with their own base, and producing **A Few Hotheads** *- a record of the 1984/85 miners strike.*

1986

Jan 20: Britain and France give go-ahead for Channel tunnel.

Jan 28: Space shuttle *Challenger* explodes soon after take-off.

Feb 7: Baby Doc Duvalier flees Haiti. Riots follow.

Feb 16: Pickets at Wapping clash with police.

Feb 25: Cory Aquino becomes new president of Philippines. Ferdinand Marcos flees to Hawaii.

Mar 5: High Court disqualifies and fines 81 Liverpool and Lambeth councillors for failing to set a rate.

Mar 29: GLC abolished.

>>

Hostile Elements

"**H**istory isn't what happens, it's what's written down and broadcast. The Chinese authorities' control of the means to propagate their distorted view of the Beijing massacre has assured the widespread dissemination of this version of events throughout China. As the victors of the battle of Tiananmen Square, they have firmly re-established their authority to write their version of events into the history books, at least for the time being.

According to the swiftly-prepared version of *The Truth About The Beijing Turmoil*, only a tiny handful of people were involved, and these were "hooligans and ruffians", who "harbour inveterate hatred against the government". "Swollen with arrogance", this small group attempted to "throw the nation into a turmoil". Much of the impetus for the protests was credited, not to the natural dissatisfaction of large elements of the Chinese people, but to "political forces outside of the Chinese mainland and in foreign countries", in order to deflect the blame from the ageing rulers. In the face of "rioters...frenziedly attacking military vehicles", "beating, smashing, looting and burning" and "savagely murdering soldiers and officers of the martial law troops", the soldiers and policemen showed "utmost restraint":

> *"To defend the motherland, the Constitution and the people, they sacrificed their blood and even their precious lives...Though they have weapons in their hands, the soldiers and officers would rather be beaten up than injure civilians accidentally."*

During the weeks of unrest, and since the massacre, the Chinese authorities have been active in distinguishing between ordinary Beijing 'citizens', who sided with the soldiers of the People's Liberation Army, and 'rioters':

> *"Risking their own safety and braving the burning fire and bricks thrown at them by the rioters, Beijing Citizens take a wounded soldier to safety".*

And according to this report, most of the students and their supporters who had camped out in Tiananmen Square left 'voluntarily'; no-one was killed during the evacuation:

> *"During the whole operation, not a single person, including the students who refused to leave, died."*

This claim is rejected by all independent observers and by the Amnesty International Report (*CHINA: the massacre of*

In October 1989, Phil Cope of Valley and Vale visited Beijing, just four months after the massacre of Tiananmen Square smashed the greatest flowering of the Chinese Democracy Movement.

This article is taken from the introduction to a Valley and Vale exhibition, consisting of photographs and bilingual text, which was closely based on an exhibition prepared by the Chinese government, entitled 'The Truth About The Beijing Turmoil', mounted - appropriately - at the Military Museum in Beijing immediately after the massacre.

June 1989 and its aftermath, 17th September 1990), in which numerous eye witnesses give testimony to "soldiers deliberately shooting unarmed citizens and military vehicles crushing people".

The Chinese authorities are also silent on the many hundreds killed away from the Square during the conflict period and on the summary executions still being carried out. According to this account, the soldiers' main task after June 4th was to clear up the mess left by the protesters, "restore order" and return Tiananmen Square "to the embrace of the people":

> *"On June 17th, ten thousand Beijing Young Pioneers gathered in the magnificent Tiananmen Square. As the first group of little guests on the square since the announcement of martial law, they and the soldiers and officers of the martial law troops jointly held a meeting, its theme being, 'We love the Communist Party and the Socialist Motherland'."*

^
Poster from *Hostile Elements*, a Valley and Vale exhibition of photographs of China after the Beijing massacre, 1990.

But while the nature of the Chinese government's propaganda response to Tiananmen Square might seem crude and unconvincing to our media-literate minds, it should not lead us to be too smug about our own position. Anyone who viewed the cynical editing of the accounts of the miners' strike by the BBC and ITV, or followed the farces surrounding attempts by our government to suppress views of Britain incompatible with their own (Peter Wright's *Spycatcher*, the *Death On The Rock* and *Secret Society: Zircon* television documentaries, the prosecution of Clive Ponting, etc. etc.) must feel less than confident that we are always getting the full story. The new Official Secrets Act (1990) has made the task of those wishing to present an 'alternative' view even more hazardous. Meanwhile, in Northern Ireland, a large section of political thought is still legally prohibited from being expressed at all.

"Anyone should be allowed to speak out, whoever he may be, so long as he is not a hostile element."

Mao Tse-Tung, 1945

In our 'democracy' which prides itself on 'freedom of speech', the degree to which criticisms can be voiced publicly is closely related to their compatibility with the views of those who control the means to disseminate them. The distorted version of history offered by the Chinese authorities in this exhibition appears both blatant and unconvincing to us, as it does to large sections of the Chinese people. The dangers inherent in the limits on our own rights to know - masked by the high degree of sophistication of our press and media - may represent an equally great threat to democracy and freedom. ▌▌

Notes from the exhibition 'Hostile Elements', 1990.

The Donkey's Ass is Reagan

"Condega is a small village in northern Nicaragua near the Honduran border, where much of the undeclared war with the US is being waged. Above the town, on a small hill, are the remains of one of Somoza's air force planes, shot down by rebels using primitive, often home-made weapons, during the final insurrection which swept away the dictatorship and established the Sandinista government in 1979.

It remains a strong dual image for the people of Condega, of the oppressive Somoza regime and the strength of Nicaraguans united in opposition; a sculpture collectively created, expressive, relevant. From one of the aircraft's wings raised between two stone columns, the village fills the undulating land between forested hills and wild, muddy river.

We spent four days in Condega during their annual festival of San Isidro. As well as the usual ecclesiastical events (the services, the slow processions of the saint's image, garlanded, through the streets) and the traditional activities of bringing the cattle into the main square, milking them and giving the milk to the children, the simulated planting of sugar cane, its cutting and distribution - the festival also concerned itself with updating and redirecting traditional ways of celebrating.

While the ceremonies of the cattle and the cane continued to have relevance to the community - the concepts of co-operation and sharing, and the grateful celebration of the earth's natural produce retaining their meaning and importance as expressions of the people's values - other aspects of the week were turned towards the more immediate concerns of the Condegans' survival in the face of the ever-present US government's aggressive policy towards them.

The first event of the festival, a wild secular procession, started from the Centro Popular de Cultura which had been the house of a commander of Somoza's National Guard during the dictatorship period. The masked procession, based on traditional characters, was accompanied by a rough and ready drum

∧ Condega festival, Nicaragua, May 1986 (Phil Cope)

The revolution in Nicaragua which over-threw the Somoza dictatorship in 1979 was an inspiration for people all over the world. The Sandinista government brought about programmes of health, literacy and education reform which reduced the illiteracy rate from over 50% to 12%, eradicated polio and reduced cases of measles and whooping cough by over 90% in two years.

By 1986, the US government had begun to respond to these successes by supplying arms and training to the contras, predomimantly ex-members of Somoza's National Guard.

This article, about festivities at Condega, and the one that follows it, 'Cutting Out The Censors', were written after the study tour to Latin America undertaken by Phil Cope and Carol Walker in 1985/6, which had a big impact on the team's work. The first looks at how traditional cultural events were adapted to suit Nicaragua's new, radical agenda. The second explores cultural responses to the brutal repression of opposition to the Chilean dictatorship.

and trumpet band. There's a traditional dance in Nicaragua - El Gueguense - developed by the Spanish, where the conquistadors ended up riding on the backs of the Nicaraguan native people. In Condega, this tradition was transformed, the rider becoming a Sandinista soldier and the donkey, wearing an Uncle Sam hat, was draped with the stars and stripes of the US flag.

<
Condega festival, Nicaragua,
May 1986
(Phil Cope)

The traditional carnival bull character, imported from the Spanish bull-ring, charged into hordes of schoolchildren, who scattered only to regroup and chase the bull back in waves like their attacks not so long ago on the National Guard; the superior numbers of the schoolchildren triumphing over the superior strength of the bull. Traditional images were being taken and given new relevance to make them useful to today's experience.

At each corner, the band would stop and a 'bomba' - or short poem - be proclaimed against Reagan, against Thatcher, for the revolution or in praise of the people's strength and unity:

^   Poster for Valley and Vale's
     La Lucha exhibition, 1987

> "Bomb, bomb, firecracker, firecracker.
> The donkey's ass is Reagan
> And the shit's for Margaret Thatcher."

Another day saw another procession, much bigger than the first, with carriages dressed with reeds, palms and mangos and pulled by oxen in celebration of the coming rainy season and of future harvests. Each of the floats, which were organised by the local agricultural co-operatives, was guarded by an armed Sandinista soldier.

The children on one float chanted 'Poder Popular' (people's power) while on another, a two-headed serpent portrayed Reagan grasping a 100 million dollar bill and Thatcher launching a rocket, as the possibilities for Nicaraguan harvests and the policies of US and British governments were graphically connected.

GLOBAL WALES

In the spaces between the processions, the services, the concerts and the games, there was time to explore the village. At the brown, fast-flowing river, women washed uniforms on large stones. On Nicaraguan washing lines, it's unusual not to see at least one piece of military green.

All around the village, at strategic points, were small muddy trenches, some with rifle cartridges discarded in them. After the rain the streets of Condega were rutted canals of mud in which young children paddled.

On the mountain sides, the trees' bright explosion and a multicoloured fallout of flowers both testified to the coming of a more prosperous season. And a nearby new settlement of homes was being built in another act of homage to the people's determination to stay and fight for a festival unaccompanied by the bombs and machine-gun fire in the distance beyond the town.

> *Tranquil now,*
> *Both knowing that they breathe together,*
> *Our daughters in their room,*
> *That the distant bombs are only thunder,*
> *And the fresh rain falling on Nicaragua.*

(From *The Country You Love*
by Mario Cajina Vega, a Nicaraguan poet)

First published in '7 Days', November 1986

LA LUCHA

*In immediate, practical terms, the contact with cultural activities in Latin America resulted in the **La Lucha** exhibition - which used posters to explore the arts and culture of Latin American countries - and the **La Lucha Festival**, which featured performers and film-makers from El Salvador, Chile, South Africa, Uruguay, Cuba, England and Wales, in a variety of community venues throughout the Vale of Glamorgan and Ogwr. The festival was documented in a feature-length video.*

*A second result of the visit was to involve people in Welsh communities in practical action on behalf of people in Latin America, and later Africa and China. This has included fundraising for The Mapocho Centre in Chile (described in **Cutting Out The Censors**, opposite) and the Centro De Cultura Edgard Lang, which develops activities with young people in Managua, the capital of Nicaragua. Funds have also been raised to establish a music wing at the Solomon Mahlangu Freedom College in Tanzania, dedicated to the memory of James Madhlope Phillips. Recently Valley and Vale have also organised a series of seminars as part of the Global Wales initiative, which aims to raise awareness about the political, social, economic and environmental factors which link Wales to the world.*

"It is not just our feeling that we, from our relatively privileged position in the West, should be supporting radical initiatives such as these, but also a sense of the importance of uniting with these groups and learning from each other."

Carol Walker
Valley and Vale

Cutting Out The Censors

"**O**n Saturday 31st January, the Clwb Ifor Bach in Cardiff was the venue for the first public showing in Wales of Duncan Campbell's film 'The Secret Society: Project Zircon'.** The BBC had been encouraged to decide that we should not be able to see this film, and the government had even concluded that it was unsuitable viewing for the nation's MPs. As it turned out, there had to be three showings that evening, each of which was packed with people expressing their belief, through this collective act of disobedience, in their right to know.

Almost exactly a year before, in January 1986, a friend and I were travelling in Chile. The 'illegal' screening in Cardiff reminded us of an evening spent in the Mapocho Centre in downtown Santiago, watching clandestine videos of Chilean news and views which had been similarly omitted from the programming of the national television channels.

Sitting down to an evening of television in Chile isn't exactly a 'Chilean' experience when one realises that what's on offer includes outdated episodes of Dallas and Dynasty, old North American movies and *El Show de Benny Hill*. With the sound switched off you could be forgiven for thinking you were watching only the worst of North American TV, as even the Chilean-made soap operas ape the white middle-class rules laid down by their US predecessors, as though the history of Chile had begun with the European invasions of the 16th century.

The same imperialist strategy dictates all TV advertising, as bland, white skinned, 'beautiful' people extol the virtues of middle-class homes and commodities, in a country of predominantly dark haired Mestizo and Indian people with an IMF debt of US$21 billion and a thirteen year old dictatorship.

Within this context, it is no surprise that the official information services offered by national TV serves no-one's interests except those of the military regime and its small, elite band of supporters. The daily eruptions of protest from every level of Chilean society against Pinochet's politics go either unreported by Chilean TV or are briefly presented as the rantings of isolated 'Cuba-sponsored' fanatics, often alongside lengthy reports of cleverly filmed official government events in which a handful of paid extras are made to look like an army of Pinochet's supporters.

The power of this portrayal of reality on the minds of the Chilean people should not be underestimated. In our

Stills from *Andreas De Victoria* by Ictus TV, Santiago de Chile.

v

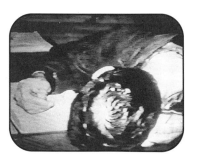

media-dominated world, the electronic image appears synonymous with reality, and events not commented upon by the media cease even to exist.

Writing about the reality of life in Guatemala, in Chile and in Brazil in his book *Days and Nights of Love and War*, Eduardo Galeano complained that "The criminals have the keys to the jails". Throughout Latin America, they also have the keys to the TV and radio stations and to the printers and newspaper offices and to most of the large-scale means of production of ideas and images.

Against this background, the work of the Mapocho Centre in Santiago, and other places like it, are of great significance. Set up in November 1981, it has had to move twice because of attacks by police and extreme right-wing brigades. It holds regular screenings, both in the centre and outside, of VHS and Betamax videos made independently in Chile, and banned feature films smuggled into the country. These are always well attended, such is the demand for a democratic information service which supports Chilean identity.

The videos shown on the night we attended included footage and commentary on the bombing of a church in

<
Democracy Rally, Parque O'Higgins,
Santiago de Chile,
Nov. 1985
(Phil Cope)

Punta Arenas, protests in a Santiago shanty town, and the mass rally staged in November 1985 in the Parque O'Higgins which brought together almost one million people in united opposition to Pinochet's misrule.

This was the news denied to Chileans by their own TV and newspaper media, the images which helped to make sense of the Chilean people's daily experiences.

The evening ended with a screening of the film *Somos Mas (We Are More)* made in Chile in 1985. It concerned the peaceful Greenham style women's protest movement, whose non-violent tactics frustrate the police and military whose only training has been to respond to aggression. It's a film which ridicules the police's violence and demonstrates - through humour - the strength of a united group of unarmed people in the face of the full paraphernalia of a fascist regime; positing in the process a different kind of society, and a different basis for human relationships.

History isn't what happens. Increasingly, nowadays, both here and in Chile, it's what gets recorded and finds the means or the permission to be screened or printed. During the Falklands/Malvinas War, Margaret Thatcher, assisted by her ally, General Pinochet, decided what should or should not be known.

Their increasingly successful attempts to build societies based upon secrecy and the manufacture of fear and division through the control of the means of producing and disseminating information are what make spy satellites like Zircon a possibility. They are also what make places like the Mapocho Centre, which are working for a different kind of future, such a necessity. ▌▌

**published in 'Independent Media',
February 1987**

>> 1986

Apr 2: Bomb explodes on board TWA Boeing 727.

Apr 15: US launches air strike on Libya.

Apr 30: Fire causes leak at Chernobyl nuclear power station in Soviet Union.

May: John Stalker is removed from enquiry into RUC shoot-to-kill policy.

May 25: 30 million people *Race Against Time* for SportAid.

Jun 12: Derek Hatton expelled from Labour Party.

Jun 16: Strike in South Africa to commemorate Soweto uprising.

Jun 20: Lambs in parts of Cumbria are not slaughtered due to fears of Chernobyl fall-out.

Jul 9: Thatcher restates opposition to sanctions in South Africa, saying they hurt black people most.

Sep 21: Prince Charles admits on TV that he talks to plants.

Sep 23: Edwina Currie says people in the North have poorer health due to ignorance.

Oct 27: De-regulation, 'the big bang', in the City of London.

Nov 30: Release of hostages sparks Irangate row.

Nov 30: Last pit closes in Rhondda Valley.

Dec 3: 4 million people apply for gas shares.

Dec 21: Chinese students demonstrate for democracy in Shanghai.

In 1986, Valley and Vale's work included **As We Were, Youth In Camera, Ourselves** *and* **A Time & A Place For Me** *- photography exhibitions, a* **Dance Festival,** *the culmination of regular dance workshops linked to visiting performers. Money was raised for a* **U-matic video edit suite** *assisting the production of* **Life In Trouble, Barry Island Rock, Garw Valley Silver** *(about the Garw's silver band) and* **The Big March** *(about the last day of operation of the Garw Ffaldau Colliery).*

The (censored) images of South Africa which reach us almost every day through our television sets and newspapers suggest a world as far removed as can be from our experiences here in Wales. But most nations in our small world are intimately connected. Most countries support or feed off each other, though these relationships are not always clear.

Wales' forced incorporation within the British state following the 1536 Act of Union made the Welsh people reluctant partners in much of the imperialist breaking and entering - including that in Southern Africa - which made Britain the economic power that it was. The cultural consequences of this ingestion were similarly disastrous both for South Wales and for South Africa.

Steve Biko writes of the African experience that:

> "Colonialism is not satisfied merely with holding a people in its grip and emptying the native's brain of all form and content; by a kind of perverted logic, it turns to the past of the oppressed people and distorts, disfigures and destroys it."

The effects of cultural domination were also well understood by Matthew Arnold, writing about Wales a century earlier:

> "It must always be the desire of a government to render its dominions as far as possible, homogenous...Sooner or later, the difference of language between Wales and England will probably be effaced, an event which is socially and politically desirable".

Arnold's recommendations were fully observed. Anti-Welsh legislation and an education system which punished those who spoke the language ensured that the number of Welsh speakers fell from 90% to 20% in the following 120 years.

Both nations are united too, by the burden of their riches: in South Wales by coal; in South Africa by coal and diamonds. The establishment and development of industries to extract both these forms of naturally-occurring carbon from the ground changed the face of both countries and dictated new and more severe orders of labour for its native populations and for those who moved to the new false promise. J.L. and Barbara Hammond report that in the 1840's, the conditions in South Wales, following the needs of this nascent industrialisation, "were

The South Wales/South Africa Festival in 1988, dedicated to the memory of James Madhlope Phillips, aimed to highlight the cultural, economic and political links between South Wales and South Africa, through a series of performances and workshops by Welsh and African artists.

Out of the festival in 1988 came an exhibition which celebrated the ways in which the people of both regions have defended themselves and their identities, particularly through music, dance and song.

Highlights of the festival were also included in a video 'Culture for Change'.

In 1990, to celebrate the release of Nelson Mandela, a second South Wales/South Africa Festival took place, which included a performance by the Soweto Youth Drama Society alongside Barry's Children and Youth Performance Group.

more like those of a newly discovered gold-field or a plantation in tropical Africa". It is still the mining industries, which, more than anything, dictate the present relationship between our two lands.

The run down of the South Wales coal industry resulted in part from the recognition that coal could be imported at cheaper prices using low-waged labour abroad, including coal produced under the conditions of apartheid in South Africa. In the early eighties, Welsh pit winding gear and other machinery was sold to the South African mining industry, and during the miners' dispute itself, South African coal was imported as a means of breaking the strike.

Likewise, in 1981, a whole steel plant from Llanelli was sold to South Africa resulting in Welsh redundancies and the importation of steel at a new lower price back into Wales. Both these examples indicate a clear relationship between the low wages and poor working conditions of miners in South Africa and growing unemployment in Wales. As Ron Webster of CPSA puts it:

"The important thing for the people of Wales to remember is that the economy which provides us with jobs is, in fact, a world economy. And multinational companies within that economy can

>> 1986

Mixed media work included Castaways, Pollution & Entering the Future - all playschemes projects - and Staying For The Sake of The Valley and A Threat and A Promise - both street events in Blaengarw.

Exhibitions also included La Lucha, resulting from the return of Phil Cope & Carol Walker from Latin America (having established cultural links with projects in Nicaragua and Chile).

Links with national organisations included roles in the Shelton Trust, the Wales Congress In Support of Mining Communities, the Association for Dance and Mime Animateurs and the Independent Film and Video Association of Wales.

1987

Jan 9: Ernest Saunders resigns as Guinness Chief Executive over shares scandal.

Jan 21: Terry Waite captured in Beirut.

Feb 12: *"Good Christians won't get AIDS"* - Edwina Currie.

Feb 22: Andy Warhol dies.

Mar 6: *Herald of Free Enterprise* sinks off Zeebrugge. 200 die.

Mar 12: Sizewell B nuclear power station in Suffolk gets go-ahead.

Apr 5: Mary Whitehouse attacks *EastEnders* for portraying low morality.

May 28: 19 year old West German lands a plane in Red Square.

Jun 11: Conservatives win general election for third time in succession.

Jul 17: Irangate hearing in US.

Aug 6: SDP votes to merge with Liberals.

Aug 19: Michael Ryan kills 14 people in Hungerford.

Sep 16: 70 nations agree on measures to reduce threat to earth's ozone layer.

Sep 24: Britain loses appeal against court decision to allow publication of *Spycatcher* in Australia.

and do take decisions which link together the destinies of our people and the people of countries like South Africa."

But there are other, more human connections and characteristics which bring together the people of South Wales with those of South Africa, and it is those that this exhibition celebrates. People whose political and economic parameters are artificially restricted to serve interests not their own will always rise up to defend themselves. In South Wales and in South Africa, a significant part of this defence has been through cultural means, and in particular, through music and song:

"Nothing dramatises the eagerness of the African people to communicate with each other more than their love for song and rhythm. Music in the African culture features in all emotional states."

Steve Biko

"The thrill of music is for us most often a physical one, in the throbbing of the larynx, the reverberations of the head, the pulsing of the blood, and the greatest thrill is that of harmonising."

Gwyn Williams

>
Shikisha,
a panel from the
*South Wales/
South Africa*
exhibition

Harmony is central to both African and Welsh music, suggesting as it does a preference which is both aesthetic and political.

"All African songs are group songs...Tunes were adapted to suit the occasion and had the wonderful effect of making everybody read the same things from the common experience."

Steve Biko

In South Wales, choirs and brass bands have led marches and performed at protests and during strikes since the Industrial Revolution changed the face of the land and its

> Dafydd Iwan,
a panel from the
*South Wales/
South Africa*
exhibition

people. Performers like Dafydd Iwan, Côr Cochion Caerdydd, The Chartists, Dave Burns and Bomb and Dagger continue this tradition of musical resistance, at the same time as linking the struggle for independence here with those in other countries. Their work, and that of others like them, defies the rising tide of cultural uniformity and demands for the people of Wales a voice in the definition of what Wales is and will become.

**Introduction to 'South Wales/South Africa'
exhibition brochure, 1989**

**INCITING THE PEOPLE
TO SING!**

One of the central figures in the musical and political history of Southern Africa is James Madhlope Phillips, to whom the South Wales/South Africa exhibition was dedicated.

James, who was exiled from South Africa because of his trade union activities used his talent for singing to campaign for the rights of his and other people of the world, up until his tragic and unexpected death in 1987.

In 1952, James Madhlope Phillips was arrested with Nelson Mandela, Walter Sisulu, Yusuf Dadoo and others for taking part in the 'Defiance of Unjust Laws' campaign. He was accused of 'inciting the people'.

*At his trial, the judge asked: "Inciting the people to do what?"
The prosecution replied: "Inciting the people to sing!"*

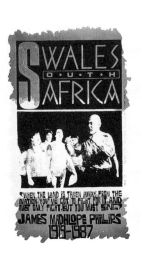

^ Poster from the first
*South Wales/South Africa
Festival*, 1988

Part 3 MAKING HISTORY

Our culture persuades us that History is a country inhabited only by a privileged few. The version of the past most often seen in the media and advocated in the school curriculum minimises the role of 'ordinary people' in its creation. The History Curriculum, for example, does not include the last 30 years, severing the past's connection with the present and with the significance of our own actions now. Meanwhile events which the media claims are 'making history' seem similarly distant from our more immediate concerns: connections are not made between dramatic, 'newsworthy' incidents and the longer social processes which create them and in which we all share. It is suggested, by this sleight of hand, that our daily lives are outside the flow of History. History happens Somewhere Else.

The effect of this version of history is to neglect and exclude the lives and actions of the majority of people. But despite this, those who are left out do have ways of recording the past, of remembering it, maintaining it and using it in the present. People are experts in the stories of their own lives; not always perhaps in the dates and timings of what happened where - facts which progressively fade over time - but much more importantly in the feelings, the attitudes and the values which illustrate and underpin the changes that have occured. Apparently insignificant memories - the personal triumphs, the tragedies, the moments of humour and of pain - can tell more about the experience of living in a particular era than volumes of dry historical fact.

Oral history draws on these memories to enable people to reveal and share aspects of the past which have been excluded from the history books. It can enable a community to value and understand the experiences upon which it is built, experiences which are often undermined or neglected.

The following article draws on Valley and Vale's work to create two 'living archives', which take as their starting point the experiences of the people of Barry and the Ogwr valleys. The aim of these projects is to enable these communities to develop a resource of images, recollections and information about

"It's time to pull up a stool by the front door and tell the story before the historians arrive."

Gabriel Garcia Marquez 'Big Mama's Funeral'

< Photo from *Domino Club:The World* exhibition, part of *The Barry Living Archive*

their own past which would make sense of the great social and economic upheavals that were and are occuring in both areas.

"A friend came to see me in a dream. From far away. And I asked in the dream: 'Did you come by photograph or train?' All photographs are a form of transport and an expression of absence."

John Berger

Oct 19: Shares crash on 'black Monday' for stock exchange.

Nov 19: 31 die in King's Cross fire.

Dec 6: Reagan and Gorbachev sign first ever treaty to cut size of nuclear arsenals.

In 1987 Valley and Vale organised its first international festival, **La Lucha***, including visiting performers Dave Burns, James Madhlope Phillips, Mayapi, Manguare, the Bristol School of Samba, The Chartists, Côr Meibion Cwm Garw and Côr Cochion Caerdydd. The festival also resulted in the production of a video,* **La Lucha***.*

Completed videos included **Staying for the Sake of the Valley***, launched at the festival and later featured in The Waste Game for BBC Wales,* **Entering The Future, Heart to Art, Tom, Dick and Barry***, and* **Now Is the Time***, a probation video that was banned from being screened by its sponsors.*

The **Video & Disability** *training workshops were established, offering basic training for disabled people in video techniques.*

Bolivian musicians **Rumillajta** *worked on a week of dance and music workshops at Llanfrechfa Grange Hospital.*

Talks included presentations at the first **Foyle Film Festival** *in Derry, in Bogside, Shantallow and Creggan estates.*

1988

Jan 3: Thatcher becomes longest continuous serving Prime Minister this century.

Jan 7: Nurses go on strike.

Jan 22: Alton's private members' bill to reduce time limit on abortions from 28 to 18 weeks sparks widespread protests.

Mar 7: 3 members of IRA shot dead in Gibraltar.

Mar 19: Wales win Triple Crown.

Mar 28: Scientists confirm greenhouse effect.

Apr 21st: Nurses win 15% pay rise.

May 23: Demonstrators invade *6 o'clock News* in protest against Clause 28.

>>

A Sense of Belonging

"The people of South Wales have always had a keen sense of history. The force of popular memory was perhaps at its strongest in the nineteenth and early twentieth centuries, particularly in communities based around a single industry like the mines of the South Wales valleys and the docks of Cardiff and Barry, where songs, stories, banners and meetings transmitted the experiences of a community from one generation to the next, and actively used those experiences to understand and shape the struggles of the present.

But the post-war period has brought with it an assault, not only on the economic and social bases of those communities, but on the cultural activities which have sustained this sense of connection with the past. The demise of the coal industry, and of the docks which provided the means to take the 'black gold' to every corner of the world, has been accompanied by the erosion of the forms of communication which shaped the collective memory. In the Garw valley, where there used to be six pits, there are now six video shops! The predominantly oral culture of songs, meetings and adult education has been ousted by newer cultural forms - television, radio, national newspapers. This is not to say that the new technologies are inherently undemocratic, or that they have in themselves changed relationships between people. But their development has been determined by the global market and the interests of central government rather than by local, communal concerns. There is less room in this large-scale, profit-led distribution system for cultures rooted in particular communities and likewise less space for a sense of history based on the needs of a specific group or geographical area. As a result, they serve to obstruct rather than express the flow of popular memory.

How we know the past depends on our sense of identity in the present. The past is filtered through our construction of ourselves (how we want to be), through what we perceive to be the prevailing values of our community, through what we have subsequently learnt. Likewise our knowledge of the past shapes our awareness and actions in the present.

> "Since memory is actually a very important factor in struggle (really, in fact, struggles develop in a kind of conscious moving forward of history) if one controls people's memory, one controls their dynamism."
>
> Michel Foucault

"We all know each others history. There are no secrets in the valley...Spread it out, it's like evangelism really, isn't it? Never lose your sense of belonging, never. Be politically aware of what's going to happen to you, how it's going to affect your future. Where are you going to find a life and how are you going to change it to the good? By clinging together and working together, being strong in that way, communal, and pass it on, down the line."

Berwyn Howells
Garw Valley Project, 1987

"The value of the Docks itself, the culture it provided, this wonderful mixed culture...There are people living on estates who probably don't know that their family originally came from another country, they don't know. Some people will wonder why didn't we ever know any of this happened, how important the Docks were to Barry. Your future's based on your past, and it's important to know these things, it really is. It isn't every town that has such a background."

Maureen Flipse,
Barry Docks Centenary Project, 1989

The broadcast and print media and the education system offer a 'national' history, not one based on the specific experiences of particular communities or classes of people. This national history tends to deny things which threaten the 'national' consensus: dissent, conflict, difference.

>
Part of
The Barry Living Archive
(c/o
Maureen Flipse)

An illustration of this process at work is the development of industrial theme parks. The central aim of the theme park is to attract tourism to areas where large scale industries have declined. Tourists bring with them their 'spending power' and - so the theory goes - give a boost to local service industries. So the theme park is designed for an audience of outsiders, and its version of history is the reverse of popular memory, which reconstructs the past 'from the inside' and in the interests of those doing the remembering. The theme park creates a version of the past which necessarily eliminates conflict, or at least the connections between conflicting forces in the past and conflicting forces in the present: conflict might make the visitors uncomfortable.

If the past is to become more than a tourist attraction it is important to develop a radically different approach. A history which enables people to understand the present does not submerge or eliminate conflicts and

>> 1988

Jun 11: Nelson Mandela's 70th birthday concert at Wembley.

Jul 6: Piper Alpha rig disaster.

Jul 6: Butler-Sloss report on Cleveland child abuse case published.

Jul 28: Paddy Ashdown becomes leader of SLD.

Sep 26: Publication of *The Satanic Verses.*

Sep 30th: Britain and Iran resume diplomatic relations.

Oct 18: Government sacks all trades unionists still employed at GCHQ.

Nov 5: Acid house party arrests.

Nov 11: George Bush elected President of USA.

Nov 17: Benazir Bhutto becomes first woman to head Moslem state.

Nov 29: Launch of *Charter 88* movement, calling for constitutional reform.

Dec 3: Warning against eating eggs because of salmonella outbreak.

Dec 16: Edwina Currie resigns over egg row.

Dec 22: 270 die in Lockerbie disaster.

*In 1988, Valley and Vale organised the **South Wales/South Africa Festival** in memory of James Madhlope Phillips, including performances by African Dawn, Bomb and Dagger, Uthingo & Amabutho, Taxi Pata Pata, Benjamin Zephaniah, Côr Cochion Caerdydd, Heavy Quartet and Shikisha.*

*A second base was established in the **Holm View Centre** in Barry and funds raised to equip it with U-matic & VHS edit suite and community darkroom.*

*The **Rock For Life** festival was organised in Bridgend in September. **Staying for the Sake of the Valley** was screened at the Edinburgh Film Festival; other videos were widely distributed.*

*The team visited and presented work in Denbosch in **the Netherlands** as part of a Welsh Festival.*

*Photography exhibitions included **Look At Us**, and a major exhibition of community photography at the Ffotogallery in Cardiff.*

>>

contradictions. A history which values local experience not only enables people to tell it in their own words but encourages the speakers themselves to decide on ways of presenting it and contextualising it.

Valley and Vale's festival to coincide with the centenary of Barry Docks, **Built For Two Ha'Pennies,** attempted to do this at a time of major change in the economic, social and cultural life of the town.

1989 marked one hundred years since the first ship sailed into what was to become, in 1913, the largest coal-exporting port in the world. 1989 was also the year in which the government abolished the National Dock Labour Scheme, ending the system which guaranteed the terms of dockers' employment. The Bill was the symbolic closure of an era in which the prosperity of town and docks was inextricably linked. In reality, this era had ended some thirty years earlier: the docks declined in tandem with the demise of the coal industry which had provided their major export. Barry's older generation, however, remember childhood in a boom town:

> "I can remember as a boy, every coal hoist was occupied. The tier was packed with steamers awaiting their turn to be loaded, with more shipping laying out in the 'roads', unable to be accommodated in the Docks themselves. Coal was being loaded right round the clock, with no let up."

> Frank Hodge

The history of the Docks is a fundamental part of the town's identity. The task of the festival was to enable local people to explore, through their own recollections, what this identity meant for a future in which the docks would employ only a handful of people as Barry's economy

"A lot of people say they used to be able to leave their front door open and never had anything taken. Perfectly true. But, on the other hand, they didn't really have anything of any worth to take."

Dafydd Davies (Maesteg), from
The Valleys Autobiography.

shifted to other more diverse industries.

Work on the festival took place over several months and the finished result included the creation of six photographic exhibitions, four videos, all made by local people, a community play involving about two hundred participants and a publication, **In Our Own Words, In Our Own Pictures.** The process involved Barry's communities in the collection and collation of a vast amount of information, memories and pictures of the town. The project gathered momentum as news of it spread from those involved to their friends and relations.

The festival had sparked a version of the past which was quite different from that found in the history books: a portrayal of the life of a town through the feelings, attitudes and experiences of those who have lived in it. The often turbulent story of the upheavals of the century emerge not as statistics or national trends, but in the details of individual and collective experience.

> Part of *The Barry Living Archive*

This approach raises its own complications. History is not an individual but a collective process. Oral history raises the problem of authenticity: we embellish, correct, simplify our stories according to how we want to appear. What emerges from oral evidence is not one history but many, diverse and changing. The plurality of oral history places a lot of weight on how the material is interpreted. In order for it to become a tool for those whose history it is, several things need to happen, beyond simply the unadulterated reproduction of interviews and photographs.

Recalling the past can itself be a traumatic experience, and a published interview can leave the speaker in a vulnerable position within their own community. When interviewees replay their own words in print or on video their instinct can be to attempt to reconstruct the material in a way they think is more acceptable. This contradicts one of the aims of oral history, which is to uncover material which has been hidden precisely because it is

1989

Jan 10: *"The Communist Party has no God-given right to rule"* - Mikhail Gorbachev.

Jan 19: Czech riot police disperse demonstration in central Prague.

Jan 20: Viraj Mendis deported from Britain despite protests.

Feb 1: Four American vigilantes set up 'The Guardian Angels' to 'police' the London underground.

Feb 2: Last Soviet troops leave Afghanistan.

Feb 3: P.W. Botha resigns as leader of the National Party in South Africa.

Feb 14: Khomeini orders *fatwa* on Salman Rushdie for blaspheming Islam.

Feb 29: Vaclav Havel jailed in Czechoslovakia for 'inciting' last month's demonstrations.

Mar 2: European countries agree to ban CFCs by the end of the century.

Mar 5: Time Inc. and Warner Communications announce plans to merge into the world's largest media empire.

Mar 7: The Palestinian uprising - the *intifada* - against Israeli occupation continues in violent clashes between Israelis and Palestinians.

Mar 23: Tanker *Exxon Valdez* runs aground spilling 11 million gallons of crude oil off Alaska.

Mar 30: Home Office publishes plans under which parents may be held responsible for juvenile crime.

Apr 1: Poll Tax starts in Scotland.

Apr 6: Norman Fowler announces abolition of Dock Labour Scheme, offering redundancy pay of up to £35,000.

Apr 15: 94 die as fans are crushed at FA Cup semi-final at Hillsborough.

Apr 17: Student protests begin in Tiananmen Square, bringing crowds of up to 100,000 people.

May 5: John Smith and Labour win Vale of Glamorgan with largest swing in a by-election since 1935.

May 13: 1,000 students begin hunger strike for democracy in Tiananmen Square.

May 17: Over a million people demonstrate in Beijing.

>>

seen as problematic and to enable people to use it to challenge assumptions about the past and present both within and outside the community.

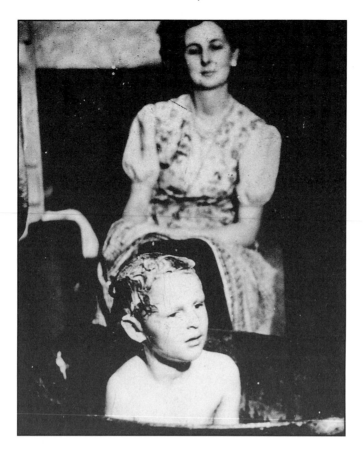

Academic oral historians have tended to respond to these difficulties by not allowing those interviewed any further control over how their evidence is used. Interviews are edited, reworked and even published without the collaboration of the speakers: oral history has been seen primarily as a resource for historians, whose role is to give the individual experience a context or to use it to support their own particular theory. It has rarely been seen as a resource for those whose experience it uses.

The aim of the Barry Docks Festival was not simply to cast light on lives which had not to date been considered worthy of documentation, but to enable a community to use its own history as a springboard for future developments, a means of exploring ideas and visions of the world. Establishing a structure through which individuals could oversee and participate in the use of their own life stories, and feel they had an ownership of and confidence in the finished product, was fundamental to this objective. The projects enabled groups of people to learn skills in photography, video making, publishing, writing and performing so that, instead of simply telling their stories and giving up control over how they were represented, they could have a central role in all stages of

"...any reflection on the past becomes, to some extent, a prophecy of what is to come."

Francisco Ayala

production.

Central to generating a feeling of pride in and ownership of the festival was that the material presented - in the form of exhibitions, performances and videos - needed to be of a quality which stood up next to the images and events people consume daily. Although the festival was about privileging the everyday experiences of the town's inhabitants, exhibited material needed to be presented in a way which wasn't everyday. The venue for the exhibitions was important in this respect: it was held in the Docks Offices, an imposing Victorian building which had been the hub of the docks administration, but which the majority of people in the town had never entered. Enabling the public to 'take over' this building to present their own story was both ironic and effective in giving the Festival a status.

The next important factor was to make explicit links with the present, not to allow the past to settle into the comfortable distance, but to ask questions about how it related to current developments in the town. This meant deliberately seeking out opinions about the present and ensuring that ideas about the future were displayed and reached those in positions of power. It also meant making links between the older and younger generations of the town, through projects which enabled young and old to work together, bringing their different experiences to make connections between past and present.

Finally, the material needed to be accessible to individuals and groups in the community for them to develop and rework it. The festival needed to have a ripple effect, as different groups took up its themes by drawing on and adding to the archive. Within the exhibitions themselves, there was scope in the form of a video box and photo reproduction facilities to add to the archive there and then.

When the festival came to an end, the question was how the town could use the resource it had produced. A new space has been found for a local history archive in The Memorial Hall in Barry. This will give the project a physical focus, and the town an additional facility from which to continue the work done around its own history. The importance of a permanent and developing archive is that it enables a community to chart its own growth and to recognise the role that people have played in the transformations of the past. Valuing that experience is the first step to empowering people to transform the future.

February 1990

May 30: Students erect 'Goddess of Freedom' in Tiananmen Square.

Jun 4: Troops surround Tiananmen Square and start shooting at demonstrators as they leave.

Jun 6: Funeral of Ayatolla Khomeini has to be abandoned because of crush of mourners.

Jun 9: Chinese authorities order round-up of dissidents.

July 1st: Police attempt to shut down at least a dozen acid house parties.

Aug 1: First phase of missiles at Greenham Common are withdrawn.

Aug 2: Cabinet approve the complete write-off of the publicly-owned Water Authority's £5 billion debt, as preparation for privatisation.

Aug: A few hundred East Germans begin to cross Hungarian border to Austria illegally.

Sep 6: Bush announces plan costing $7.86 billion to halve drug use in US by year 2000, saying: *"Drugs are sapping our strength as a nation"*.

Sep 16: Thatcher vetoes plans to mount the most comprehensive survey of British sexual habits ever.

Sep 20: 300,000 people in Scotland have failed to pay the Poll Tax. In Glasgow, one in three adults has defaulted.

Oct 3: East German authorities impose ban on visa-free travel to Czechoslovakia after thousands seek refuge in West German embassy in Prague.

Oct 16: After a week of public protests, Eric Honecker abdicates in East Germany.

Oct 19: Guildford 4 freed after 14 years in jail.

Oct 26: Nigel Lawson resigns.

Nov 9: Berlin Wall comes down.

Dec: Thatcher defeats Anthony Meyer in Tory leadership contest.

Dec 14: Chilean elections end Pinochet's 16 year dictatorship.

Dec 24: United States invades Panama to oust General Noriega.

Dec 29: Vaclav Havel elected President of Czechoslovakia.

>>

Part 4 TAKING CONTROL

In the last ten years, a growing 'disability arts movement' has begun to assert the identity of 'disabled people' and has played an important role in placing their rights on the national agenda.

Central to this has been the use of the arts to enable people to explore and give voice to their experiences, from their own perspective, and above all to call into question the notion of disability itself. Disability is a social construction based on ideas of what is or isn't normal: the less a person functions as a 'normal person', the more disabled they are deemed to be. The problem with this definition is that it creates artificial and oppressive norms that need not apply, and so explains disability as an individual medical problem, and not a problem to do with the way society is organised. Photographer David Hevey has argued for a radically different understanding of the term:

"My definition of disability is of people who are systematically segregated from society...It is a civil rights issue. There are certain medical conditions which are physically fixed, but the disability is the social counter-engineering, the negative response to it. The disability is the strip lighting or the three steps up into the building."

Stereotypes of disabled people as freaks or sinister or pitiable or brave have pervaded television and radio, the press, comics, children's books, sideshows, films and literature. Representations of disability have rarely been created by disabled people themselves.

These stereotypical images have been given more weight by the fact that the patterns of disabled people's lives have been segregated from the mainstream. Despite the fact that one of the government's first education reforms in 1981 included a commitment that most disabled children should be educated in the same schools as other children, today four out of five remain in special schools. The welfare system compounds this: the lifestyles of the majority of disabled people are determined by a series of institutions - the day centre, the residential hostel, the hospital.

"The celebration of difference...is the celebration of humanity."

Vic Finkelstein

56

< An image from *Self Portraits*, Bridgend Day Centre, 1989

Disabled people have, historically, had little control over the decisions and policies of these institutions. This lack of power and of independence has meant that they have rarely had the opportunity to explore identities which differ from those offered by a disabling world, from the portrayals of tragic figures whose lives are wholly dominated by difficulties. Even to be eligible for benefits people have to show the extent to which they fit the value judgements and definitions of the medical profession!

Film-maker Chris Davies has written that:

> "Able-bodied people act on the assumption that since we are always to be dependent on them, control of the images of disabled people naturally should be in their hands...Self-image and self-projection are not common to the experience of most disabled people. I too was handicapped by the assumption that I was to be forever dependent, a pale shadow of the able-bodied people around me."

This pattern is beginning to change as disabled people gain greater access to the arts and media, reflecting on and speaking out about issues which concern them. For people who live in institutions, however, attempts to voice their ideas often face the entrenched attitudes of the bureaucracies which surround them. Partly this is because, as disabled people begin to develop a distinct cultural identity, and as they call into question the notion of disability that is so broadly held, they pose a threat to the way in which these institutions run, indeed to their very existence. The project described in 'Whose Portrait Is It Anyway?' ran into just such a conflict. 'A Trade In Wind', which describes a project which took place outside an institutional setting, is a more positive example of how the arts can open up new possibilities both to explore identity and to have an input into the choices made about our lives.

>> 1989

In 1989, Valley and Vale began work on the **Living Archive for Barry,** an ongoing 'people's history' project launched with **Built For Two Ha'Pennies** - the Barry Docks Centenary Festival.

The Festival included the production of 4 videos including **All Change For Barry,** a **community play** in the Barry Memorial Hall, exhibitions **History Is Pictures, Out Of The Blue, Wish You Were Here** and **Land, Sea and Sky.** There were **performances** by the Kafala Brothers, Ebony Steel Band, Dafydd Iwan, Orquesta Reve, Benjamin Zephaniah, Shikisha and the Tredegar Town Band.

Valley and Vale **Sell Out,** a trading subsidiary to market the products of community arts projects, was established with a part-time worker.

Other video work included the production of **A Trade In Wind** and **Culture for Change** - about the cultural and economic links between people in South Wales and South Africa.

Photography projects included **Self Portrait** at Llanfrechfa Grange and **Self Portraits** at Bridgend ADC.

The **Valleys Autobiography** project was launched with **The Promised Land** - a video about people's memories of the Ogmore Valley,

1990

Jan 1: Glasgow begins year as Cultural Capital of Europe.

Jan 12: Gorbachev visits Vilnius in Lithuania amidst growing unrest in Soviet republics.

Jan 13: 50,000 people demonstrate in London in support of ambulance workers.

Jan 18: Gorbachev sends Red Army into Azerbaijan following clashes between Azeris and Armenians.

Jan 22: Yugoslavian Communist Party votes to abolish its leading role.

Feb 2: De Klerk lifts a thirty year ban on the African National Congress and the South African Communist Party.

Feb 20: A draft law allows republics to break away from the Soviet Union after a simple referendum.

Feb 11: Nelson Mandela released after 26 years imprisonment.

Feb 25: Pro-democracy rallies sweep Soviet cities.

Whose Portrait is it Anway?

If you take a photograph of yourself, you don't usually have to ask permission to show it to other people - unless you're labelled 'mentally handicapped'. In which case the people who control your life - hospital administrators, consultants, social services, parents - also control your image.

The **Self-Portrait** exhibition was the result of a photography project organised by Valley and Vale in Llanfrechfa Grange, near Cwmbran. Llanfrechfa is a residential hospital for people with learning difficulties; the project aimed to provide a medium through which eight of the residents could explore the making and selection of images of themselves. Making decisions can be a difficult hurdle for people who have spent their lives in institutions, and the project began by exploring the fundamental skills necessary to make choices in photography: recognising yourself in a photograph, understanding differences in posture, what you wear, where the photograph is taken, the expression on your face, framing. These skills are taken for granted by people who use photography regularly, as part of the language of their daily lives.

Using a cable release, the group were able to become both photographers and subjects at the same time. We established a darkroom facility in the hospital, enabling participants to develop and print their photographs. To reinforce decisions, we set up a number of cognitive games: identifying pairs of different sized copies of the same photograph, and choosing between prints. The sixty or so self-portraits which the group selected to become the exhibition are the product of this decision-making process, and as such they make a clear, tangible statement about their creators' perceptions and abilities.

The exhibition was shown at the hospital, launched before an audience of residents, staff, parents and guests. It was then set to be shown to a wider audience beyond the institution, touring nationally and also to the Netherlands, where it had been included as part of a festival of work by people throughout Wales. In the week that it was due to leave, two consultants at the hospital decided that the photographs could not be shown. The reason given was the the exhibition did not represent a 'positive view' of people with a learning difficulty. This judgement took little account of the fact that the photographs were taken and developed by the residents themselves, who, in most cases, had selected them as their favourite images. In preventing the exhibition from being shown, the hospital authorities effectively said they did not believe the

In 1989 an exhibition of self-portraits, produced by a group of people with learning difficulties, was prevented from being shown outside the hospital (at which they were residents) by the institution's administrators. This article was written as an immediate response to the ban and attempted to look at some of the issues it raised.

Due to the continuing ban on the exhibition, the photographs used here are not from Llanfrechfa Grange, but part of a similar exhibition completed in the same year by people at Bridgend Day Centre.

residents capable of making their own choices on such issues.

It is a strange view of positive images, that they should be defined by medical staff and not primarily by the residents themselves. Any attempt to change society's misrepresentations of disability must involve enabling people who have been marginalised in this way to speak for themselves, to create their own images. If these images are sometimes uncomfortable, perhaps we need to question whether what is conventionally accepted as a positive image is often an assimilation of the subject into the 'normal' world. 'Positive images' have the potential to mask real oppressions, and so perpetuate them.

>
Images from
Self Portraits ,
Bridgend Day Centre,
1989

The authorities at Llanfrechfa went further, suggesting that people with learning difficulties shouldn't be making self-portraits at all. "They do not have an integrated self-concept" explained one of the consultants. "They should take pictures of animals, birds, traffic, cars, flowers - interesting things."

Our society confines people with a learning difficulty in institutions, in language, in diagnoses, and it is assumed that they are incapable of thinking for themselves. Descriptions throughout modern history - 'idiot', 'defective', 'retarded', 'subnormal', 'mentally handicapped' and even 'learning difficulties' - fix people to a disability rather than a capability: 'the verbal dustbin to which my child is confined' as one parent put it. Active participation in the community by those labelled in this way is prevented partly because their abilities are underestimated; this is done by institutions as well as individuals.

At the end of the nineteenth century, fears of a declining national intelligence led to the establishment of colonies and asylums, usually situated a few miles from major towns, as part of a policy of segregation. Up until 1971, children with 'severe learning difficulties' were legally excluded from education and from the provisions of the 1944 Education Act. People with 'learning difficulties' are not sick, but many remain segregated in hospitals. As the decision at Llanfrechfa Grange shows, medical staff still

Feb 26: Sandinistas defeated in Nicaraguan election by US-backed National Opposition Union, headed by Violeta Chamorro.

Feb 28: 18 Oxfordshire councillors resign Tory whip over Poll Tax.

Mar 5: A week of violent demonstrations across Britain against Poll Tax ends in riot in Brixton.

Mar 10: Iraq sentences *Observer* journalist Farzad Barzoft to death for 'spying'.

Mar 11: Lithuania declares itself independent.

Mar 18: Right-wing Alliance for Germany wins clear victory in the first East German election.

Mar 22: Teaching union, NAS/UWT, says a survey of teachers shows that they work an average 51 hour week, with administration taking up 28 hours, mainly due to the new National Curriculum.

Mar 24: Opinion poll gives Labour a record 27 point lead over Conservatives.

Mar 25: Estonia votes to break with Moscow.

Mar 28: Luke Rittner resigns as Chief Executive of Arts Council over government plans for arts funding.

Mar 31: 300,000 people take part in Poll Tax demonstration in London, which ends in riot. 300 arrested.

Apr 1: Riot in Strangeways prison, Manchester.

Apr 11: Parts of a 'supergun' intercepted on their way from Britain to Iraq.

Apr 11: It is reported that the number of people who have developed AIDS as a result of heterosexual intercourse has nearly doubled in a year.

Apr 25: Anti-abortionists fail in attempt to reduce time limit on abortions from 28 to 18 weeks.

May 4: Mandela has talks with De Klerk.

May 11: Inflation hits 9.4%, the highest for 8 years.

May 15: Agriculture Minister John Gummer eats a beefburger with his daughter - in front of reporters - as evidence that B.S.E. ('mad cow disease') does not present a risk to public health.

>>

have considerable control over even non-medical areas of the lives of the residents. "We know our residents totally", claimed one of the consultants.

>
from
Self Portraits,
Bridgend Day Centre,
1989

As Joanna Ryan writes *in The Politics of Mental Handicap:*

> *"Medicine - its institutions, personnel, concepts and modes of explaining behaviour - has been the main instrument for excluding mentally handicapped people from society. It is not just that hospitals have had to cope with people whom society has rejected, which is how many nurses and doctors see their role. It is also that the medical profession has sanctioned this rejection by producing a whole way of thinking that justifies it."*

The relationship between photography, medicine and learning disability has both supported and contributed to this way of thinking. The invention of photography in the mid-nineteenth century was taken up by the pioneers of physiognomy and psychiatry because, as Dr. Hugh Diamond argued, the camera could record "with unerring accuracy the external phenomena of each passion, as the really certain indication of derangement". In an age when the 'outer man' was believed to be a 'graphic reproduction of the inner', photography became an important tool in diagnosing mental handicap, sometimes even a substitute for visiting the 'patient'.

Photography projects in 'Adult Training Centres', special schools and hospitals are beginning to reverse this history, enabling people with learning difficulties to show that they are not 'totally known' by others, but have a need to make their own decisions about the way they are represented. This is true not just in photography, but in a wider context, and institutions should and often do act to safeguard and promote self-advocacy by those in their care. Unfortunately, the consultants at Llanfrechfa claimed they had no knowledge of the long history of work on developing self-image with people with learning difficulties.

Self-Portrait was finally allowed a limited showing. The majority of parents of those involved supported the project, and a curtailed tour was seen as a compromise. Several panels were missing from the exhibition because a number of parents decided their sons and daughters should not be included. Whilst it is clearly important that parents should be allowed to argue for the interests of people with learning difficulties, this right must be questioned when their decisions undermine the autonomy of those individuals. None of the creators of **Self Portrait** are children, and the decisions they made about the exhibition were taken in a supportive and responsible environment.

Present thinking about the organisation of services and facilities for people with 'learning difficulties' is centred on the ideal of community care. Hospitals like Llanfrechfa now pursue progressive policies of 'normalisation'. It is the stated aim of community care that provision should be made for people with disabilities which enables them to lead 'as normal an existence as possible'. Included in this is the belief that they should participate in the organisation and control of their own care. This policy will not be carried out successfully if the choices made by clients are dismissed by staff who are supposed to be providing that care. Institutions have an important role to play in the process of empowerment, in enabling their clients to gain more control over the course of their lives. Projects like **Self-Portrait** are a small step in this direction because they enable people with 'learning difficulties' to begin to define who they are and what they feel. These definitions become influential when they are seen widely: a touring exhibition can change attitudes and become a platform for discussion about the organisation of services. In deciding to withdraw the exhibition prematurely, the hospital authorities will make its creators invisible again. ▮▮

first published in 'Llais', November 1989

A WORLD OF DIFFERENCE

A World Of Difference is a video by three people with physical disabilities, made with the help of Valley and Vale.

"We hope this video will challenge the prejudiced views of some people which arise from a combination of a lack of understanding of and misinformation about disability issues.

Our aim in making the video is to promote the needs of disabled people, to educate and to challenge our audience.

We want change which enables us to live and participate as fully as possible in a society which has marginalised and restricted us."

Robert Higgins, participant

A Trade In Wind

"The video, 'A Trade In Wind' was made by two people who have experienced mental health problems. The aim of the project was to explore and raise awareness about mental health issues using video. 'Madness' is a cultural, social and political definition which needs to be publicly questioned by those who find themselves on the wrong side of it.

As one of the participants said:

"Until recently, people labelled as 'mentally ill' have had little or no say or control over their lives and treatment in mental hospitals, and have been put into the position of being passive partners, with no control over their destinies, as our lives have been totally ordered and controlled by the psychiatrists and governing bodies that run these institutions."

The project began by using discussion and role play to explore the experiences of people in the group and their contact with mental institutions. Participants then learnt basic skills in video production to enable them to turn these ideas into a short video, which has since been used by them to initiate debate about the participation of psychiatric patients in the planning of mental health services and to campaign for their right to discuss their own treatment.

Gaining technical skills and having editorial control over the video was a crucial feature of the project. The views of those who have experienced mental health problems are increasingly being sought by broadcasters and the makers of training films on mental health issues. Whilst this is to be welcomed, it is not a substitute for real power over the production of those programmes, over how their views are presented. Too often, interviews are used to give the appearance of consultation, in programmes which do not challenge the marginalisation of users' views in the planning of services.

The process of screening the video was as important as the process of producing it, as it allowed the group to communicate their ideas to people who are often remote and inaccessible to those they are supposed to serve: administrators, policy-makers, trainers and broadcasters. Each screening was introduced by the makers of the tape and followed by a discussion with them about the issues it raises. As well as giving the group confidence this also gave them a forum to put across a users' perspective to mental health professionals. A short video operates as a

The idea for the video 'A Trade In Wind', came from a group of people who wanted to voice their views and experiences of the mental health system. Meetings for the project took place in participants' homes and a local community centre, rather than as part of the programme of a hospital or day centre. In this respect, the project reflected an attempt to move towards a situation in which disabled people have more control in planning and developing cultural activities, instead of 'receiving' them, a situation where those cultural activities address the real and pressing issues affecting the lives of a group, not the interests of the institutions they inhabit or even of the arts organisations they work with.

useful trigger to debate and puts its makers on a more equal footing with the articulate professionals who play such a significant role in their lives.

The group has travelled throughout South Wales, Britain and even to an international conference in Rome, showing the video to self-help groups, mental health workers, students on social science courses, general practitioners, art therapists and TV producers. At these screenings, the video has enabled them to put their own experiences on the agenda, to start the long process of overcoming the power imbalances - between therapist and 'client', between administrator and 'patient', between those whose work requires the use of labels and those who are labelled.

extract from article first published in 'Mediawise', Spring 1990

"It was like being in the military on male A ward: 6 am rise and shine; dressed if behaving, but otherwise kept in pajamas; constantly being observed; being woken up to be given sleeping tablets. And so it goes on, day after day, week after week."

Eddie Somers
(one of the makers of *A Trade In Wind*)

May 21: Labour Party warns members not to support All Britain Anti-Poll Tax Federation, calling it a 'Militant front organisation'.

May 28: Albanian football team steals £2,000 worth of goods from duty free shop at Heathrow.

May 30: Yeltsin voted in as President of Russian republic.

Jun 3: SDP disbanded.

Jun 21: Police set up a four mile exclusion zone around Stonehenge to prevent people gathering for summer solstice.

Jun 27: British Aerospace agree to repay sweeteners paid by government when it bought the Rover group.

Jul 22: Riot police raid acid house party in Leeds and arrest 836 people.

Jul 26: Thatcher speaks at European summit against plans for a single European currency and a central bank.

Aug 2: Iraq invades Kuwait.

Aug 8: American and British send troops to Saudi Arabia.

Aug 16: *"We shouldn't have had all these campaigns to get the Birmingham Six released if they'd been hanged"* - Lord Denning.

Aug 23: Western hostages shown on TV with Saddam Hussein.

Sep 17: Iraqi diplomats expelled from Europe.

Oct 8: 21 Palestinians shot dead by Israeli troops during rioting in Jerusalem.

Oct 12: Debate on Europe splits Conservative party conference.

Oct 25: Polly Peck International, one of Britain's top 100 companies, goes bankrupt.

Nov 1: Geoffrey Howe resigns over Thatcher's opposition to European monetary union: *"I believe I can no longer serve with honour."*

Nov 2: B.S.B. merges with Sky to become part of Rupert Murdoch's media empire.

Nov 14: Michael Heseltine announces he'll challenge Thatcher for Tory party leadership.

Nov 22: Thatcher resigns.

Nov 27: John Major becomes new Prime Minister.

>>

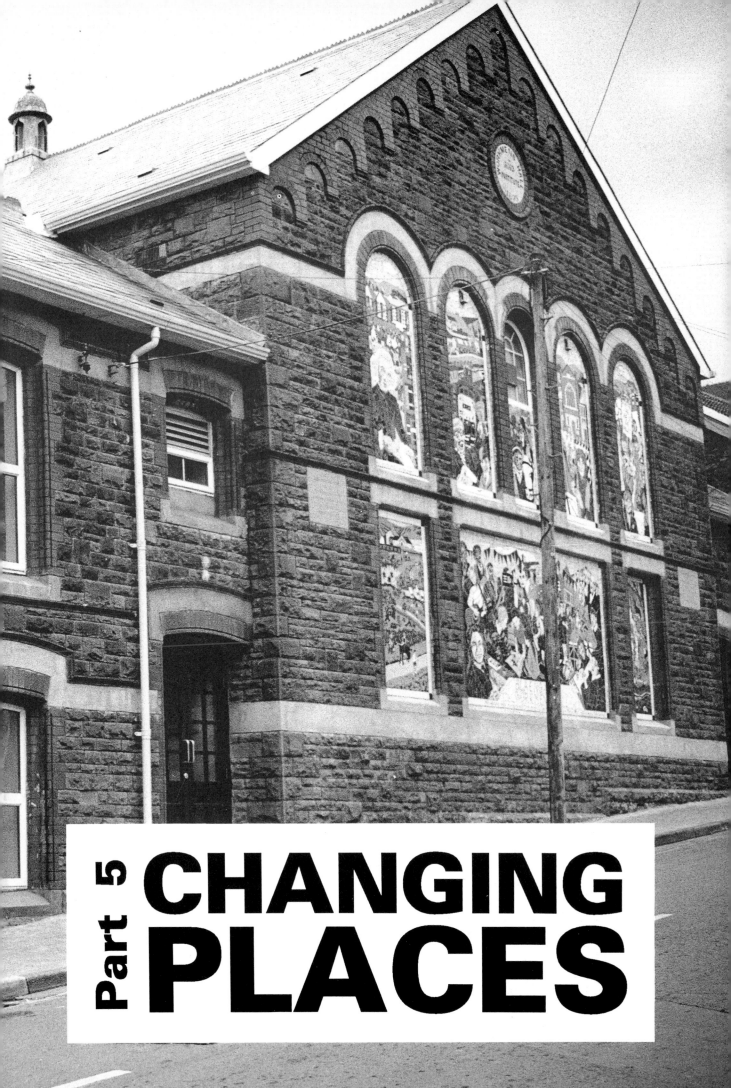

Part 5 CHANGING PLACES

CHANGING PLACES

Community arts claims to be a means of effecting change, of empowering people to participate more fully in society by enabling them to explore and communicate their ideas. The success of the movement as a whole, much less any single community arts project, in relation to these claims is not easy to evaluate. The last ten years have seen an inexorable move away from collective values and towards those which emphasise the individual. We are a long way from developing a democratisation of culture let alone a democratisation of society.

Alternatives to the predominant consumerist culture in Britain have rarely succeeded in firing the popular imagination. Recent radical thinking about society has come almost exclusively from the right wing of British politics. The Labour Party and Trades Unions have seen their role as 'breaking' rather than making images, vacating a territory which was once their own: what Raymond Williams, described as 'the sense of what any of this liberation is for, the sense of what the struggle would be to attain, the sense of what human life would be, other than mere Utopian rhetoric.'

The arts offer a space within which 'the sense of what human life would be' can be felt and thought. Attempts to link cultural work to practical change need to explore how that sense can be nurtured, not separate from, but alongside political and social developments. There is a need to reconnect artistic activity to the concerns of a community, to see it as a means of that community's development, a way of thinking creatively about problems and of exploring new directions.

These concerns are not only cultural. They will include the physical infrastructure of a place, health, welfare rights, crime, the environment - the whole spectrum of experience in late twentieth century society. The arts can play an important role in stimulating people to express their needs and aspirations and in encouraging them to participate in the developments affecting their community. As such, they are a crucial tool in any attempt to broaden local democracy.

< Renovated Blaengarw Workmen's Hall, April 1992 (Garw Junior Photo Workshop)

●

"Without vision a nation perishes...Without
vision a village perishes...I believe we are more
than just people who can use tools, people who
are able to communicate with one another.
There is an inner part of us that needs
sustenance and food, and oftentimes that is
given to us as the result of cultural activities...
I think it was Herman Goerring who said
'Whenever I hear that word culture, I reach for
my gun.'"

Vernon Chilcott (Bettws),
part of *The Valleys' Autobiography*

>> 1990

Dec 6: Iraq agrees to free Western hostages.

Dec 20: Maerdy colliery, the last pit in the Rhondda, closes.

*1990 was the first year of Valley and Vale's **Three Year Action Plan**, and saw the consolidation of two major **Living Archives** in Barry and Blaengarw. Activities included the completion of **In The Same Boat**, a video about the Thompson Street area in Barry, one of the first multicultural communities in Britain, and **For Bettws or Worse**, involving people in Bettws in planning facilities in their community.*

*'**A Trade In Wind**' was shown at L'Arte Costa Del Drago festival in **Rome**, presented by Eddie Somers, one of the people who made it.*

*The **South Wales/South Africa II** festival in June/July celebrated the release of Nelson Mandela with performances by Thomas Mapfumo and the Blacks Unlimited, The Kafala Brothers, Dave Burns, Edward II and the Red Hot Polkas, Shikisha, the Milkshakes and Barolong Seboni. The festival featured the **Soweto Youth Drama Society** performing 'Where Is My Son?' alongside **Barry's Youth & Children's Performance Group**.*

*Involvements in other organisations included a role in **Global Wales**, the **Valleys Initiative for Adult Education, Community Enterprise Wales** and the **South East Wales Community Arts Forum**.*

1991

Jan 11: Soviet troops fire on civilians in Vilnius, Lithuania.

Jan 17: Gulf War starts: first air attacks launched on Baghdad.

Jan 18: Iraqi Scud missiles hit Israel.

Feb 13: Up to 500 Iraqi civilians die after an air-raid bombs Baghdad shelter.

Feb 16: *"Iraq is like a special operations theme park"* - General Schwarzkopf.

Feb 24: Land war starts in Gulf.

Feb 28: Iraqis withdraw from Kuwait.

Mar 6: It is reported that 950 oil wells are on fire or damaged in Kuwait.

Mar 14: Birmingham Six released after 16 years.

>>

CHANGING PLACES

Building For The Future

"**Following the miners' strike, communities in South Wales were faced with widespread pit closures. The last pit in the Garw Valley closed in December 1985. To mark the end of over 100 years of mining in the valley, 2,000 men, women and children marched from the pit gates through the streets of Blaengarw.**

It rained so hard that the planned burning of the National Coal Board flag had to be abandoned because it refused to light. Instead, angry feet trampled it into the ground. Even the weather seemed to be on the side of Thatcherism, robbing the miners of their last, defiant gesture. The day was full of hopelessness and anger.

One of the consequences of the defeat of the strike was a prevailing disillusion with traditional forms of communal action. Correspondingly, the priorities of Valley and Vale were shifted from work in support of specific campaigns towards stimulating a broader debate about the future of the region. There was a clear need to re-build a belief in the value of collective participation in the affairs of the community. Eight months after the pit closure, another march took place from the pit gates through the streets of Blaengarw, but this time with a different mood. **Staying for the Sake of the Valley** was a street event devised and staged by young people of the Garw, which was the culmination of easter and summer playschemes projects run by Valley and Vale.

The project began with discussions and questionnaires to establish a theme for the event. Central to the children's experience of living in the valley was the recent pit closure and its effect on the community. Most were clear that they wanted to stay in their community rather than join the increasing numbers of people moving away in search of jobs and 'better opportunities'. However, strong feelings emerged about the kind of environment and opportunities they wanted in the valley, the things that would enable them to stay. This became the focus of the project: **Staying for the Sake of the Valley.** The team ran workshops in banner-making, construction, drama, dance, music, song-writing and poetry, with all the groups working towards the final event.

On the day, despite more rain, hundreds of local people turned out to watch the performance. The event began at the pit gates in Blaengarw with a dance/drama piece based around a large-scale replica of the winding gear, and moved on to process through the streets. The procession was joined at various points by a 'drum train' playing home-made instruments, and characters with huge heads representing aspects of the valley's future. The event culminated in the dismantling of the 'winding gear' which was reassembled into giant letters spelling the word 'STAY'. This was followed by a live performance by the music group playing songs written especially for the event.

By voicing their hopes for the future, young people had begun to make their desires conscious in the community. Following the event, some of the participants wanted to develop these ideas further, working on a video which took up the theme of the playscheme. They interviewed local residents and argued the urgent need for the community to take on board the aspirations of young people in an area which by now had no industrial base, poor recreational facilities and was witnessing large-scale youth migration to towns and cities. The video asked the question 'Why should young people stay in a place which seemingly has so little to offer them?' As with the street event, the video powerfully stated the desire of its makers to remain; it looked at the immense cultural richness of the valley, and argued that the survival of the community depended on a transformation of the opportunities it offered the young.

The video was shown in the Garw Valley Centre to a large audience and the screening was followed by a sometimes heated debate about the lack of facilities in the area and the reasons for it. The future of Blaengarw Workmen's Hall emerged as a key concern. The discussion that followed was the starting point for a community initiative to raise funds to redevelop the Hall as a facility run by and for local people.

This development was particularly significant in the light of the history of the building. The Blaengarw Workmen's Hall and Institute was built in 1894, paid for by voluntary deductions from miners' wages. A penny in the pound for six years amounted to the £1,200 needed.

The Hall provided a focus for social, cultural and sporting activities. It was used for meetings of all kinds and was later altered to include cinema projection.

The Hall closed its doors as a cinema on Good Friday 1976, when a gas leak poisoned a packed house of adults and children. Since then, the building had steadily deteriorated, until none of it was fit for use by the public. Valley and Vale had moved into the Hall in 1986 and used the building to run workshops in dance, drama and video, as well as an administrative base for its outreach work, despite holes in the windows, no heating and

"The last train is going and it's never coming back. The buses are being privatised and my dad's got the sack. We're staying in this valley You can hear us shout We're staying cause we want to, Not cause we can't get out!"

^
Still and song lyrics from the video
Staying for the Sake of the Valley

"We want work with decent pay We want somewhere for the kids to play You can wash coal dust off with soap But you can't wash away our hopes."

69   *CHANGING PLACES*

mouldy walls.

Following the video screening and a number of public meetings, a plan to renovate the Hall was developed, coinciding with the Welsh Office launching its 'Valleys' Initiative' scheme. The proposal was put to the Welsh Office, and nearly one million pounds was raised under the scheme, a quarter of which came from the local borough council, Ogwr. Raising this money was a major triumph for the valley: the next step was to find ways of ensuring that the Hall's redevelopment reflected the needs of the community, and that there was local participation in the design and control of the new building.

Between 1987 and 1991, the plans for the Hall became the major focus of the team's arts projects in Blaengarw. Playschemes involved young people in thinking through and articulating their ideas for both the building and the valley as a whole. A large-scale oral history festival, **The Valleys' Autobiography,** looked at the role the Hall had played in the life of the area and how this might relate to its refurbishment. Projects such as these provided a mechanism whereby those living in the valley, and particularly young people, contributed their own aspirations for the building: a process of consultation which ran much deeper than the occasional public meeting or brief display which usually characterises attempts to 'get the views of the public'.

Out of this activity emerged a plan by which the Hall would aim to fulfil a number of the valley's needs, whilst retaining its character as a cultural centre. The new building would once again contain a flexible 35mm cinema and theatre space, a community surgery and cafe, alongside a sound recording studio, video, desktop publishing and photographic facilities, as well as general purpose rooms and an adminstrative base for Valley and Vale.

<
New Land for Old,
Garw Junior Photo Workshop,
August, 1991

After two years of building work the Hall opened in December 1991, a significant development of the physical infrastructure of the valley. Whilst not all of the original proposals were implemented, due both to the inflexibility of the fire officer and lack of funds for capital equipment, the Hall is substantially what was dreamt of before the Valleys Initiative came along. Already, the photographic workshop has produced a book, **Land**, there are dance, drama and DTP workshops for all ages, there have been music and theatre performances, packed cinema audiences and work has started on a large-scale community play.

A unique feature of this revival had been the involvement of the community in planning, stimulated by the sequence of arts-based projects which enabled local people to voice their needs. The success of the initiative points to the contribution community arts can make in galvinising community action and creativity. Perhaps most importantly of all, the cultural work helped revive a sense of ownership of the building and an active participation in decisions about the future of the valley, experiences which will be important in ensuring that the Hall continues as a vibrant focus for the community's activities.

February 1992

a book of photographs
by children from the
Garw Valley

LAND

In April 1989, Valley and Vale and Ogwr Groundwork Trust formed an ongoing partnership under the banner **Garw Land**. Involving more than 100 local young people between the ages of seven and twelve, the scheme aims to raise interest in the environment of the Garw Valley and to document, highlight and learn from the present day aspects of the landscape through the medium of photography.

In this short time, groups of Garw children have created seven exhibitions - **Up A Mountain**, **Up A Mountain In The Rain**, **Up A Mountain In The Snow**, **The Long March**, **Off The Rails**, **Water** and **New Land**. These reflect a time of great change in the Garw Valley, literally through the eyes of local young people, from the demolition of the last pit to the reclamation and redevelopment of the same sites. All the photographs were taken, developed, printed and selected by children themselves, to reflect their views of the way their world is changing.

This is not, however, yet another document of industrial decay. **Land** is primarily a celebration of the often overlooked but frequently stunning landscape of the Garw - conducted with a vision and technical standard that stands with any neighbour on the bookstore shelf. In November 1991, the book was launched, income from which will assist the development and extension of the project.

A Different Kind of Animal

"**M**arket forces have not been kind to South Wales. In the 1870's and 80's the demands of England's manufacturing industries ravaged the South Wales valleys for coal, disregarding the indigenous farming communities. When the same manufacturing industries were forced into decline in the 1970's and 80's, the mining communities were just as quickly abandoned.

The new, 'light' industries which are to some extent replacing the traditional employers, continue to act as the old coal industry did, moving in and out of Wales as their financial needs dictate, as conditions and benefits change. If they can bring prosperity to an area overnight, they can and do as quickly take it away again. As Eastern European countries are opened up for investment, creating an even cheaper and potentially more pliant workforce, this instability will increase.

It seems a bleak environment in which to look for possibilities for change. What is there within this new landscape that can be used to shift the agenda away from the concentration of power that 'market forces' inevitably require? What are the opportunities to shift the balance towards a greater accountability, towards a more widespread democracy?

One significant way in which communities have responded to declining local industries, unemployment and the closure of local amenities is to establish locally-controlled organisations which provide goods and services vital for their survival. One such example of 'community business' was set up when the main supermarket closed in Blaengwynfi in West Glamorgan, leaving nowhere in the area to buy food and groceries: a group of local people formed a co-op and took over the building on behalf of the community, starting a successful supermarket of their own, which also provides much needed jobs. Elsewhere, a Credit Union, run on a non-profit-making basis by local people, offers savings facilities and low interest loans to people who would otherwise be prey to loan sharks.

As a member of Rhondda Community Business put it:

> "What it's about in this local community is we want to stop people mucking us about, basically. Before we do this we have to be independent...I see it as a link with a hundred years of working class self-activity, of working people organising their own lives."

72

Valley and Vale's distribution arm, **SellOut**, is an attempt to translate this principle of local ownership into the work of a community arts organisation. SellOut is constituted as a separate (though wholly-owned) entity from the main arts team and functions as a community business to distribute the products created by local people on Valley and Vale projects. The impetus behind the venture was a desire to distribute more effectively the ideas and views contained in the videos, photographic exhibitions, writing and other work produced by community groups. At the same time, the proceeds from sales are used to part-fund further work. At the time of writing, Valley and Vale is also exploring, with a number of different community groups, the possibility of establishing community businesses based upon video, photography and sound recording activities which could operate from within the Blaengarw Workmen's Hall.

In some ways it is a dangerous path to tread. Community businesses must not allow themselves to be seen as a substitute for state funding: this is as inappropriate in the arts as it is in the health service. However, they can act to supplement income and to give the organisation a degree of economic and artistic independence from the demands of specific funders. Most significantly, they can provide a means of the community developing greater control over the fulfilment of their needs - whether this be the need for a local shop, or just as importantly, the need to tell their side of the story through a video or an exhibition.

However, if these new initiatives are to avoid reproducing the low-wage, exploitative enterprises that South Wales continues to experience, attaching the word 'community' to the word 'business' must change the way the whole operation behaves. The business world is a world of transactions whose primary guiding principle is profit: the profit of the company rather than the benefit of the people who work in it and who need its goods. A community business needs to be a different kind of animal, in which the relationships between people making these transactions need to be adapted to a new set of values: it is this understanding of community which must be at the heart of any attempt to rebuild from the economic and social devastation faced by many areas at the beginning of the nineties.

The word 'community', of course, has many different applications and usages. In some ways it is a meaningless term, hardly ever used negatively, and often tacked on as an adjective to make practices and institutions seem more palatable: the 'community police', the 'care in the community' scheme, even the 'Community Charge'. Often, we use the word when we really mean an area or

>> 1991

Mar 23: Tories outline plans to abandon Poll Tax.

Apr 6: Reports of more than two million Kurds fleeing Iraq.

May 21: Rajiv Gandhi assassinated.

May 21: Plan to ban American pit bull terriers following another attack on a small child.

June: Yugoslavia heading towards civil war, as fighting increases in Slovenia.

July 6: *"All Serbs should be ready for war"* - Slobodan Milosevic.

Aug 8: John McCarthy freed in Beirut.

Aug 19: Coup in USSR ousts Gorbachev.

Aug 21: Soviet coup fails and Gorbachev returns to Moscow.

Aug 29: Soviet parliament suspends Communist Party.

Sep 3: Riots in Cardiff, Birmingham and Oxford.

Sep 5: Soviet deputies vote to dissolve USSR.

Sep 13: Riots spread to Tyneside following 'joyriding' incident.

Oct 2: Military take-over in Haiti.

Oct 8: *"The A.N.C. is unfit to govern"* - De Klerk.

Oct 17: Four ITV companies lose franchises. Thatcher apologises personally to Bruce Gyngell, head of TV-AM.

Nov 5: Robert Maxwell dies at sea.

Nov 19: Terry Waite freed in Beirut.

Nov 15 Tottenham 3 cleared of Broadwater Farm murder.

Nov 28: UN backs plan to send peace-keeping force to Yugoslavia.

Dec 7: Maxwell's media empire collapses after revelations of disappearance of Mirror pension fund.

Dec 31: Gorbachev resigns as Soviet Executive President.

*In 1991, the **Blaengarw Workmen's Hall** re-opened (in December) after two years of renovation.*

a neighbourhood. But 'community', as we are defining it, is not so much a place as a set of relationships based upon shared values and co-operation: people-based and people-centred activity.

It is this notion of community that has been so under attack in the past decade. The drive behind the Conservative legislation of the 1980's was the view that 'society' could be reduced to the sum of individual needs; that, in fact, as Margaret Thatcher said "There is no such thing as society; there are only individuals and their families". The philosophy of 'market forces' - as the mechanism through which these needs are supposedly expressed and satisfied - has no conception of the social, the collective, the communal, of 'community'.

In South Wales there is still a residual understanding of and longing for a different set of values, so evident during the miners strike, which revealed such depths of empathy, mutual support and co-operation. But if we intend to build some of these experiences and definitions of community into a brighter future, we are setting ourselves a substantial challenge. In making the needs, hopes and aspirations of local people central to business activity, organisations need to develop accountable structures through which

<
Logo for *Open for Business*,
a video and resource pack for
community groups,
produced by
Valley and Vale and Hugo Perks,
1990

communities can decide what goods and services they really need, including those in the 'cultural industries'. This will involve an assessment of the consequences of production, marketing, distribution and disposal of products which goes beyond profit and loss: issues of employment practice, protecting the environment and avoiding exploitative advertising need to be high on the agenda - something that ordinary businesses rarely take into account at all.

An authentic community business, however, in encouraging new, collective business practices can itself help recreate a sense of community - retraining (or perhaps just reminding) people of the benefits of working together, for each other, rather than under the prevailing, ultimately counter-productive, ethos of self-benefit.

At present, the pressures upon us suggest a completely different message, one which teaches that the only struggles left are personal ones, that the collective doesn't exist. As one of the participants in a community business in the Rhondda recognised:

> "The bottom line is that we've got to be organised in a way that enables us to achieve things collectively. One or two groups won't achieve anything, but to be properly organised gives you a different picture."

The possibility of communities running their own federations of community businesses, providing a series of independent, self-controlled and mutually beneficial alternatives to the kinds of employment practices South Wales has suffered in the past (and still experiences today), is profoundly liberating. Such organisations may not replace BP or Sony or Ford, but they can provide some significant examples of people-centred ways of operating - which can have major implications both for the local economy and for building a more effective democracy. ▌▌

**published in
'Community Enterprise Wales Newsletter',
February 1991**

>> 1991

*Video productions included **The Domino Club**, **Alive & Kicking**, a history of rugby in the Ogmore Valley, and **A World Of Difference**, three accounts of disability.*

***Land**, a book of children's photographs of the Garw Valley, was published and photos from it were featured in The Independent and The Guardian.*

*Valley and Vale's **tenth birthday** celebrations included two dance performances.*

1992

Jan 11: Second round of Algerian elections is cancelled by the government because of the likely victory of the Islamic Salvation Front.

Jan 15: Yugoslavia recognises the independence of Slovenia and Croatia.

Feb 1: First US-Russian summit takes place.

Mar 17: A whites-only referendum in South Africa gives a mandate for De Klerk's reforms.

Apr 9: Conservatives win surprise fourth successive election victory; polls had predicted a hung parliament.

*In 1992, Valley and Vale has developed work connected with the re-opened Hall, including **DTP workshops** for all ages and youth photography, video and performance workshops.*

*Dance and drama work focussed on the build-up for the community play which will be part of **Valleys Live '92**.*

***IndepenDance,** an integrated dance project was established in Barry.*

*There are plans to publish two books connected with the Living Archive projects, **The Valleys' Autobiography** and **Barry Changes**.*

*Other publications included the production of **Creating Meaning**, a book of articles written about Valley and Vale's work and ideas over the last decade, launched at the AGM alongside a performance by Benjamin Zephaniah on June 20.*

EPILOGUE

Two powerful and opposing currents are at work in Western industrialised societies. The first is the drive towards centralised power, towards a homogenous culture assisted by political and technological developments which make possible the global movement of goods, information and money. The second, contrary force is the demand for more localised decision-making, for extended democratic control over government and for the recognition of regional and culturally-specific identities.

In Britain, we are living in the aftermath of a social revolution. The restructuring that has occurred in British society since 1979 has attempted to make 'market forces' the governing principle of public life. The process of transforming public institutions to make them available for purchase, sale and profit, has extended to areas which, a decade ago, would have been thought beyond the reach of the market. Despite John Major's attempt to represent a 'caring Conservatism', Thatcherism - a profoundly centralising force - is still working its way through the system.

An integral part of this programme has been a shift of power from local to central government and an erosion of institutions which provided important checks to the powers of the state and the interests of corporations: the ongoing restructuring of local government, legislation against trades unions and the Education Reform Act have all extended central government control and curtailed forums for opposition to national policy. The privatisation of industries such as gas, electricity, water and telecommunications, has made possible the exploitation for private profit of fundamental public needs.

Many of these changes have been presented as an extension both of individual choice and of the accountability of public institutions: the 'choice' of school by parents, the 'choice' between private and public health care, a 'choice' of companies to provide you with a telephone, the 'choice' not to be in a trade union, and, most recently the 'Citizens Charter'. A closer look at the consequences of this legislation reveals that it has left us with, at best, little real control over the services concerned. Instead, it has resulted in a shift in the organising principles of these institutions, so that rather than provide services based on need they have turned those services into saleable commodities, and so reverted to a tiered provision which favours those able to pay the most: the survival of the fittest and richest.

In the rest of the world, similar forces to concentrate and

< *Sticks and Stones*, street event, Llantwit Major, November 1983

centralise power are at work. Multinational companies now organise both their production and markets on a world scale, the same products becoming available throughout the globe, transcending national boundaries. Organised world trading has existed since the 18th century, but new information and communications technology has intensified it, eliminating the barriers presented by time and space to corporate expansion.

Meanwhile, in the political sphere, the New World Order proclaimed by President Bush looks remarkably like the old, in which Euro-American interests are perpetuated through military and economic means. The collapse of the Soviet Union has left the United Nations and other major world organisations effectively dominated by the US. As the east-west divide crumbles, we are left with an ever-widening split between north and south, in which 6% of the world's population consume half of its resources.

The failures of centralisation, of the 'global culture', are increasingly evident: in the erosion of local and collective identities, in the pervading lack of interest in the political process in Western countries, in the vast inequalities between the West and the so-called Third World, and within Western countries themselves.

At the same time, there exists a clear desire for different, more equitable ways of organising societies, for greater regional control, for the recognition of specific cultural identities. These needs are expressed in the painful break-up of the Eastern bloc (a reaction to an equally oppressive centralisation) and, closer to home, in the renewed interest in devolved governments for Scotland and Wales.

Such needs are not being satisfied by ever larger units of social organisation, by world markets and transnational corporations. Neither are they assuaged by the superficial freedoms of consumer choice or by the expressions of difference afforded by niche marketing. A devolution of political, economic and cultural power is required which brings greater autonomy to networks of smaller and more accessible units within a larger planned whole. This is not to glamorise the local, or to deny the necessity of planning and organisation on a global scale. Local structures are not an alternative to global ones. The two are inter-related. The challenge is to embody, within global political and economic structures, a system of decentralised democratic control exerted through local participation.

EPILOGUE

If we are to begin to shift the balance of power away from the pervasive domination of impersonal forces such as 'the market', the multinational company or an introverted 'nationalism', to build new forms of community, we will need to create structures which both acknowledge and celebrate differences, but which can also find ways of communicating and uniting to achieve common aims.

Cultural activity has a critical role to play in this. In Wales and Scotland, for example, it has been largely through cultural means that people have asserted their need for greater self-determination. Our culture, and within that culture our artistic activity, our creativity, is how we form identities and become part of communities. Access to the resources to create culture is fundamental to discovering and communicating who we are. Raymond Williams has said that "the process of communication is in fact the process of community."

Without the popular control of culture, there cannot be full democracy, there cannot be functioning communities. At present, access to participation in the 'process of communication' is unevenly distributed. The one-way traffic of the dominant culture sustains forces hostile to the very notion of 'community', in order to preserve the power of a minority.

This book has shown an attempt by one small group to begin to redress this imbalance in a relatively limited geographical area. There have been a number of significant successes: the stimulation of locally-controlled economies, the involvement of people in decisions about local planning, the new voices given to people whose identities have been marginalised.

But, to have a significant impact on the nature of culture and communication within our society, there needs to be many more such locally-accountable systems of production and distribution. The arts are a crucial means of exploring ourselves and our communities, and their relationship to a larger whole. As such they have an important role to play in bridging the gulf between global and local, in bringing about a more equal distribution of power and wealth.

The year 1992 has witnessed the launching of three major multi-million pound cultural events which strongly suggest movement in a direction contrary to that argued for here.

80

In Ebbw Vale, an area of derelict land has been transformed by a £20 million reclamation scheme which has successfully removed the scars left after the closure of the local steelworks. Within the Garden Festival which has been planted in its place, however, the version of Wales that is provided is one of a "Land of magic, myths and legends, ancient rituals, fiery dragons...from primeval swamps to poetry readings, majestic castles to industrial artefacts and allotment gardens."

And near Paris, we are being told that another "dream has come true", as the Disney Corporation has exported its panoply of characters and values to EuroDisney, where you can "Stroll down small-town America's memory lane", "Whoop n' holler in the wild, wild west!", "Set sail to distant lands!", "Voyage to galaxies beyond imagination" and "Experience The Future", leading the writer George Steiner to ask "will developed Europe emerge from the seductions of Disneyland...will it find ideals of freedom, of leisure, of expanded education, which are not those of a second-rate America?"

And in Seville, between April and October 1992, the last Universal Exposition of the twentieth century, and the biggest yet with 111 participating countries, is underway. It provides in some ways the most accurate reflection of the three of what we are or perhaps of what we want to be.

Almost without exception, the national pavilions are dominated by the glossy sales pitch of the sponsoring companies, as country vies with country to produce the most spectacular multimedia presentation and the most futuristic building in which to house it. The British Pavilion, which might in the past have focussed its attention on Beefeaters, double decker buses and the British pub, celebrates the virtues of Coca Cola GB, The London Docklands Development Corporation, Thorn EMI, EuroTunnel, The London Futures and Options Exchanges, Apricot Computers, Rover Cars, United Distillers and Marks and Spencer, as the power to define Britain is handed over to the highest bidder and the lowest common denominator.

The prevailing message of Expo '92 is the continuous and unstoppable 'progress of Mankind', a seamless progression stretching back to the beginning of time and far into the future. Although this linear version of world history might be questioned by millions of the world's less fortunate inhabitants, and by the evidence of the damage done to the environment by technological 'advances' ('Progress includes progress in the art of destruction' - Octavio Paz), it certainly cannot be denied that we have reached a moment in the planet's history when the degree of sophistication of our technology and communications systems makes it possible to entirely eradicate poverty, hunger, inequality and oppression.

The challenge for the future, however, will be less to do with whether the world will continue to develop technologically - refining our ability to create and destroy - or the pace at which this will take place, but rather whether these developments will remain the property of a relatively small proportion of the world's population whose beliefs are dedicated to widening rather than bridging the gap between haves and have-nots.

And it is the energy with which 'ordinary people' and communities participate in this debate which will determine the degree to which a truly democratic and fulfilling future will be created.